If In Crisis:

1. Start at "CONTENTS," page vii.
2. Scan for relevant chapters.
3. Read "Keys" at chapter's end.
4. Read PEACEMAKING, entire chapter, page 96.
5. Think; pray; meditate; discuss.

If seeking a—
New Couple,
New Marriage,
New Life:

1. Read "The New Model of Love," in IDENTIFY, page 3.
2. Take test in "WHAT'S THE STATE OF YOUR UNION?", page 11.
3. Finish reading IDENTIFY, page 1.
4. Jump to last page of your favorite chapter; read "Keys;" scan entire chapter.
5. Think; pray; meditate; discuss.

Otherwise:

1. Read IDENTIFY, page 1.
2. Scan INDEX, page 204.
3. Scan GLOSSARY, page 201.
4. Flip to any chapter, section or page; read.
5. Think; pray; meditate; discuss.

Also by the authors:
The New Couple

WHAT'S THE STATE OF YOUR UNION?

INSTANT RELATIONSHIP SELF-DIAGNOSIS

Seana McGee & Maurice Taylor

MOYER BELL
Kingston, Rhode Island & Lancaster, England

Published by Moyer Bell

Frist Edition

LIBRARY OF CONGRESS
CATALOGING-IN-PUBLICATION DATA

McGee, Seana, 1954- and Maurice Taylor, 1960-
What's the state of your union: instant relationship
self-diagnosis
—lst ed.

p.   cm.
1. Man-woman relationships. 2. Couples 3. Marriage
4 Love
I. McGee, Seana. II. Title.
HQ801 .M33   2007
306.81076 222   2006-035515
ISBN: 978-155921-362-2 (pbk. : alk. paper) CIP

Printed in the United States of America.

Distributed in North America by:
Moyer Bell, 549 Old North Road, Kingston, Rhode Island 02881,
401–783–5480, www.moyerbellbooks.com
and in the United Kingdom, Eire, and Europe by:
Gazelle Book Services Ltd., White Cross Mills, High Town,
Lancaster LA1 1RN England,
1–44–1524–68765, www.gazellebooks.co.uk

This book is dedicated to
children everywhere, with the
hope that their parents practice
the principles contained in these pages.
May all homes truly
become the havens of love,
safety and trust that is the birthright
of each and every little one.

CONTENTS

CONTENTS

To begin with let's assess the STATE OF YOUR UNION—your committed relationship with the person you hope to be with forever—and then consider the information and tools to make right any glitches that the assessment reveals.

Before we get to those elements of assessment and remediation, though, we want to share with you the thinking that undergirds them. In our day, a truly successful relationship seems well-nigh miraculous, yet human beings don't yearn for anything that isn't possible. As a very wise person once said, miracles don't really exist; they're simply phenomena ruled by laws of nature that our scientists have yet to discover. When we started teaching, training, and counseling couples as a team—which was also just about the moment we met—we were already convinced that such natural laws must also exist for love, that there must be a way for everybody to have emotionally and sexually deep connections that last. And we embarked on a singular quest to find those laws.

To tell the truth, it wasn't only for our clients that we began our search for the most cutting-edge information and the most effective, enduring-results-producing techniques (though serving couples was, and still is, our joint mission in life). We were also bound and determined to do everything in our power not to let the gift of our own precious love fade away. Thus, inspired both by professional research and ethics and by the passion between us, we became adamant about figuring out this thing called committed monogamous relationship and discovering the laws that govern it.

The Traditional Marriage Model

The first thing we concluded was that the traditional model of marriage and relationship that we inherited from our parents no longer serves people well.

Based on the compelling but ultimately destructive myths of the male provider and the good wife and mother, that model promises safety, belonging, continuity, and everything comfortable and known. While traditional marriage accommodates our "lower-order" needs—namely, the needs for food, shelter, physical safety, and a sense of belonging to our tribe—it ignores the "higher-order" needs that define our very humanness: the need to learn to love ourselves, the need to find and fulfill our true life's work, and the need for authentic, ongoing emotional connection with another.

When we exalt the trinity of self-love, mission in life, and emotional intimacy in our own relationships, we are, perhaps for the first time, synthesizing in a practical way our individual prerequisites for happiness with those of relationship. This is couple potential in its rawest form: rather than threatening our individuality, committed relationship can actually enhance it—even launch it—and reveal to us our own true power and the full range of our gifts.

Although many of today's partners are well above the survival level of existence and are already actively engaged in meeting high-

2

er-order needs, that task becomes exceedingly difficult once we're mated with another. And though so many of us yearn to transcend the war between the sexes in order to come together in a new and authentic way, and are willing to work hard in our relationships to achieve emotional intimacy, these goals, too, elude us.

Our research and our years of working with individuals and couples have led us to conclude that partners who fail to enshrine as part of the symbolic marriage contract the development of self-love, mission in life, and true emotional intimacy can expect to pay in the currency of their own psychological and spiritual well-being—and risk becoming another depressing statistic.

Naturally, this isn't the first era in which couples have felt the emergence of more evolved needs. People in our parents', grand-parents', and even ancient forebears' times had the dubious pleasure of these urges as well; it's just that they didn't acknowledge them and couldn't address them. But now we've hit a kind of critical mass: for more people than ever before, addressing the higher-order needs is no longer optional.

The New Model of Love

It soon became clear to us that the *way* we were seeking would have to be part of an overall model of love that not only honored these more sophisticated requirements for relationship, but also boldly replaced the traditional. As the larger picture came into focus, the exact dimensions of this model—what would later become the *laws*—vividly revealed themselves in the negative: in other words, we noticed certain facets of relationship the neglect of which consistently got couples (ourselves included) into trouble. Conversely, we also noticed that a respect for these facets— each of which was integrally connected to one of the higher-order needs—seemed to help keep couples healthy. Though ignoring one facet alone was often enough to do a couple in (and respecting one alone was never enough to save them), partners were usually tripped up by a cluster of them. Though they wore many faces, these standard couple conundrums always boiled down to some variation of the following:

- ❖ Lack of a passionate initial connection
- ❖ Unwillingness or inability to prioritize the health of the relationship
- ❖ Inability to deal with emotions
- ❖ Inability to listen from the heart
- ❖ Entrenched unfairness
- ❖ Inability to make peace and restore broken trust
- ❖ Seemingly irreconcilable points of conflict
- ❖ Undiscovered or unmanifested life purpose for one or both partners
- ❖ Emotional or financial dependencies
- ❖ Unwillingness to embrace healing and education for the relationship

THE NATURAL LAWS OF LOVE

To our delight, we realized that each of these problems was linked to a binding principle. In those principles lay the essence of what we sought—THE LAWS OF LOVE.

And since none had been specifically articulated in previous generations, we call them the "Natural" Laws of Love—and called a couple who strives to follows these laws a "New Couple". The laws follow:

CHEMISTRY, the first Law of Love, refers to those indescribably special energies we feel with our true beloved. Composed of great sexual and friendship connections, chemistry provides the juice and synergy that all partners need to get through the rapids of relationship.

PRIORITY, the second Law of Love, represents our commitment to keep our chemistry alive by doing the "work of relationship" and by weeding out unhealthy preoccupations.

EMOTIONAL INTEGRITY, the third Law of Love, involves our commitment to maintain our relationship as an "emotional safe zone." It asks us to take responsibility for the full deck of our emotions and to examine—and endeavor to heal—any emotional blind spots, buttons, or issues that cause either one of us strife.

DEEP LISTENING, the fourth Law of Love, involves hearing each other straight from the heart. It represents our willingness to learn how to listen to our partner's words (and the feelings underneath) with compassion.

EQUALITY, the fifth Law of Love, is about self-respect and fairness. Though differences exist between all partners, this law asks us to be open to discussion when either one of us feels that things are out of balance or unjust, and to do something about the situation if necessary.

PEACEMAKING, The sixth Law of Love, involves our commitment to keep the peace and restore trust every time it's broken. This law entails having explicit bottom lines, acknowledging the nuclear power of anger, and knowing how to manage anger.

SELF-LOVE, the seventh Law of Love, asks that we work toward valuing, validating, and accepting ourselves no matter what—and that we clear up any unfinished emotional business from childhood that's being played out in our relationship.

MISSION IN LIFE, the eighth Law of Love, represents our commitment to discover and fulfill our life purpose, our ultimate and exalted adult job, and to be sure that our partner does, too.

WALKING, the ninth Law of Love, involves our resolve to work to clear up any emotional and financial dependencies that keep us from feeling autonomous and free within the relationship (and thereby keep us from enjoying true interdependence). Being willing and able to "walk" if need be is the best guarantee that a couple will stay *truly* together.

HELP, the tenth and final Law of Love, represents our commitment to go outside the couple to learn and heal if ever we get stuck on any of the first nine laws.

You can use these Natural Laws of Love to assess the state of your union and, where you discover problems, to work toward a healthier relationship. Questions follow this introduction that will allow you to test your New Couple potential.

Codependence and Stages of Relationship

Two dynamics of committed monogamous relationship that pertain to every law—and that will be mentioned throughout this book—are the developmental stages of relationship and the notion of codependence.

While relationships always represent an intense learning curve, most of us eventually realize that the grandest lesson is not how to love another person (though that's grand indeed), but how to love ourselves. In fact, What's the State of Your Union? assumes that every human being on earth, aware of it or not, is hard at work on this project. The nitty-gritty of raising our self-love requires that we reverse two unhealthy tendencies: the first, to place others' needs before our own; and the second, to seek acceptance from others before we accept ourselves. These particular forms of emotional dependence fall under the unglamorous rubric of codependence.

The newly enamored among us might feel at cross-purposes with the goal of self-love, believing that the objective in true partnership is for us to become less "selfish." But this is a misguided understanding of both self-love and selfishness. Just as flight attendants instruct us to place the oxygen mask over our own face before we assist our dependents, we must pay proper attention to ourselves before we can be of any real good to anyone else. True and healthy love of oneself is the bedrock of authentic emotional intimacy, which is why it's earned the distinction of being both a higher-order need and a New Law of Love. Because self-love is learned—or, more accurately, diminished—in childhood with early caregivers, poor self-love can be unlearned in adulthood with our intimates. Happily, committed romantic relationship is a great vehicle for this endeavor—so long as our beloved other is of the same philosophy and is dedicated to the same goal.

The second dynamic has to do with the progression of relationship. Love's journey isn't static; it's a process that consists of three distinct and absolutely predictable stages. Couples either progress through these or, like so many of our ill-prepared traditional foremothers and forefathers, get stuck somewhere in the middle. We call these stages of love "intoxication," "the power struggle," and "co-creativity."

The intoxication stage, which lasts roughly two weeks to two years, is a high and memorable time for most partners. These are our days of wine and roses, when the mere prospect of seeing the face or hearing the voice of our beloved is capable of producing a thrill. For many of us, this is the only time we let ourselves lapse into a fantasy of being in and feeling unconditional and perfect love. The ultimate anesthetic, this first stage of romantic love has the power, at least temporarily, to blot out the pain of our insecurities and imperfections—hence its bittersweet name.

Nevertheless, the intoxication stage of relationship ends; and it's supposed to end, as night replaces day, though few of us accept this fact. Instead, we confuse what's really an ephemeral state with true love and blame ourselves or our partner for its dissolution. That's why it's impossible to overemphasize the need for couples to expect the passing of this period, to prepare for the onset of the second stage, and to be assured that much greater things are in store.

Traditionally, the second stage of relationship—power struggle—has gotten a bad rap, characterized as either a war zone or an occupied territory. It's been so confounding for so long that it's come to be seen as synonymous with romantic commitment itself. And yet, of course, it isn't. The power struggle is just a phase—something we all go through, like adolescence and the terrible twos. The problem in previous generations was that most couples didn't have the luxury of the education or tools to "resolve" this touchy phase of relationship. That meant it went on—as it still does for many of us—till death or divorce.

On its surface, the power struggle is just that—the point in a relationship when, no matter how much each of us would like to deny it, those dreaded conflicts start to emerge. Unfortunately but predictably, the euphoria of oneness and complete acceptance erodes, we "get used to" each other, and dissatisfaction seeps into a crucible that might once have seemed impenetrable. Though to the unenlightened among us, this second stage may seem like a dirty trick, this isn't the case. For whether we know it or not, the power struggle has surprisingly little to do with our mate. Rather, it's predominantly a flashback, a further act within the incomplete drama of our younger years, which has found in our adult relationships a second stage upon which to enact itself. Once we recognize and learn from this fact, the power struggle can become the most healing and empowering period in our adult lives, enriching our significant relationships.

New Couple Work

Certainly, the passage of time alone never transports any of us out of the middle stage of relationship. Still, this stage can be brought to a conclusive and beneficial end. In fact, the bulk of this book is dedicated to teaching partners how to do this—how to move on, as soon as possible, to wondrous co-creativity. The way out is always through, which in this case means committing to the Laws of Love—that is, to the "work of relationship."

That work involves learning a basic relationship skill set and undertaking two ongoing processes. The skills are these: emotional literacy, which includes emotional awareness and fluency; deep listening; anger management; conflict resolution; and negotiation. The processes are individuation, which involves becoming emotional peers with the members of our family-of-origin, and resolving transference, a kind of ghost-busting, which entails interrupting our unconscious tendency to try to work out with our partners unresolved early relationships with our primary caregivers. Together, these skills and processes are the nuts and bolts of this book.

The work of relationship is never entirely over: all couples are works in progress. Still, it gets much easier—and the "wow of relationship" that a couple experienced during intoxication returns in a more mature and enduring form. Partners who commit to the Laws of Love will find that the power struggle yields to co-creativity; interdependence becomes reflexive and a greater peace prevails in the relationship—yet never at the price of passion; emotional intimacy becomes their way of life together; their ability to love and honor self and other expands; their individual missions are firmly on the march; and (if they have children) they present a role model of genuine partnership—a union in which each partner not only loves and respects but also openly champions the other.

If you're ready to commit to pole-vaulting out of the power struggle with the help of the Laws of Love, a soft landing in co-creativity is just ahead. As you create a life you love with the love of your life, you will be able finally to celebrate both your priceless individuality and a stellar connection.

WHAT'S THE STATE
OF YOUR UNION?

The following questions are typical of those we ask partners in therapy with us. They will form the core of your self-diagnosis. The way you answer the questions will give an indication of what law (or laws) you need to focus on.

After the quiz comes the analysis. Your answers will diagnose your potential as an individual and as a New Couple. Each chapter presents one law and the many ways of applying it to your self and your union. Although each law builds on the next, they are interdependent—functioning as a net, rather than a ladder— which means that they need to be applied concurrently. The only exceptions are chemistry, which is a prerequisite to the following nine, and help, which is the fail-safe mechanism for the whole system.

Each partner should answer these questions separately. Check the yes or no box for each of the following . If you're currently working on the issue addressed by a particular question—whether in a class or program, in therapy, or in a support group—check yes for that question.

	Y	N

1. Do you routinely share your most important thoughts and feelings with your partner? ☐ ☐

2. Do your two bodies seem to love each other independent of your minds? ☐ ☐

3. Do you tell your partner your greatest secrets and your greatest shame? ☐ ☐

4. Are you managing your work hours so that they're not a problem in your relationship? ☐ ☐

5. Are you managing your use of food so that it's not a problem in your relationship? ☐ ☐

6. Are you managing any use of addictive substances and compulsive behaviors so that they're not a problem in your relationship? ☐ ☐

7. Are your relationships with friends, ex-partners, and colleagues sufficiently straightforward that they present no problems in your relationship? ☐ ☐

8. Are your relationships with family members sufficiently straightforward that they present no problems in your relationship? ☐ ☐

9. Do you regularly level with each other about how you feel toward each other? ☐ ☐

10. Do you let your partner know when you're feeling guilty or overly responsible about anything, particularly the relationship? ☐ ☐

11. Do you let your partner know when you're feeling self-blaming or ashamed about anything, particularly the relationship? ☐ ☐

12. Are you able to label appreciation, gratitude, admiration, and love at the moment you experience them? ☐ ☐

13. Are you able to label fear, sadness, and anger at the moment you experience them? ☐ ☐

14. Are you able to tell your partner these same feelings in such a way that he or she can hear and accept them?

15. Do you feel heard by your partner well enough that you're confident he or she could accurately represent you to a third party?

16. When your partner talks to you about matters that are important to him or her, are you especially attentive?

17. Do you and your partner carve out special time at least once a week to share what's really going on for you?

18. Do you both feel that the way money is earned and managed in your relationship is fair?

19. When you think of all the day-to-day duties and responsibilities of your life together—including those relating to finances, the household, your social life, relationships with parents and extended family members, childcare and education, and maintenance of car and yard—do you feel that they're divided fairly between the two of you?

20. Have you openly discussed with your partner how any differences in gender, age, race, ethnicity, income, and financial status make you feel?

21. Have you openly discussed with your partner how any differences in talent, career, educational status, and advantages of upbringing make you feel?

22. Do you two consistently, either on your own or with facilitation, resolve conflicts until all resentment is dissolved?

23. Are you able to tell your partner when you're feeling angry, irritated, frustrated, or resentful without being aggressive, disrespectful, or frightening?

	Y	N
24. Are you able to tell your partner when you're feeling angry, irritated, frustrated, or resentful without shutting him or her out?	❏	❏
25. Have you clearly expressed to your partner that violence, verbal abuse, and sexual betrayals are unacceptable to you?	❏	❏
26. Have you clearly expressed to your partner that substance abuse and other self-destructive behaviors are unacceptable to you?	❏	❏
27. Are you two able to effectively negotiate and make deals to handle areas of conflict?	❏	❏
28. Are you aware that the most confounding issues with your partner relate to the most confounding issues with your parents, siblings, and others you grew up with?	❏	❏
29. Are you able to stick up for yourself with your partner?	❏	❏
30. Are you able to stick up for yourself with your friends and colleagues?	❏	❏
31. Are you able to stick up for yourself with your family members?	❏	❏
32. Are you aware of, and working on, your areas of low self-esteem?	❏	❏
33. Do you trust and follow your intuition?	❏	❏
34. Are you doing work that's deeply fulfilling and contributes to the greater good?	❏	❏
35. Are you supporting your mate to do work that's deeply fulfilling and contributes to the greater good?	❏	❏
36. Do you feel that you have the inner strength to leave your partner if your baseline conditions for relationship are violated and outside help has been refused or has failed?	❏	❏
37. Are you as an individual able to support yourself financially in a lifestyle that's acceptable to you?	❏	❏

	Y	N
38. Do you consider yourself emotionally independent?	☐	☐
39. Are you willing to pursue whatever educational and healing options are necessary to keep unresolved issues and conflicts from damaging your relationship?	☐	☐
40. Are you willing to pursue whatever educational and healing options are necessary to raise your self-esteem, if low self-esteem threatens your relationship?	☐	☐

Your New Couple POTENTIAL

Partners should total their yes responses separately, then combine them for a New Couple sum.

🐦 If your sum ranges between 80 and 69, congratulations! You're a stellar New Couple—and a wonderful role model for others. This book will help you deal with any future glitches, safeguard your success, and give you a language to describe what you're already doing so well.

🐦 If your sum ranges between 68 and 57, congratulations! You two are well on your way to becoming a New Couple. This book will help you get all the way home and actualize the New Couple model of relationship, give you a language to describe that model, and help you safeguard your success.

🐦 If your sum ranges between 56 and 45, you definitely take your relationship seriously. This book will teach you how to slough off those cobwebs of tradition and actualize the New Couple model of relationship, give you a language to describe that model, and help you safeguard your success.

🖤 If your sum ranges between 44 and 33, you're valiantly battling the trance of tradition. This book will teach you how to break the trance and actualize the New Couple model of relationship, give you a language to describe that model, and help you safeguard your success.

🖤 If your sum ranges between 32 and 21, you're succumbing to the trance of tradition, although you're fighting back from time to time. This book will be your welcome wake-up call. It will teach you how to break the trance and actualize the New Couple model of relationship, give you a language to describe that model, and help you safeguard your success.

🖤 If your sum ranges between 20 and 0, you're firmly under the spell of the trance of tradition. Let this self-diagnosis serve as a wake-up call to a life of much greater love and happiness. This book will help you break the trance and actualize the New Couple model of relationship, give you a language to describe that model, and help you safeguard your success.

Your New Couple WORK

If you answered no to questions:

🖤 1, 2, or 3, pay special attention to CHEMISTRY, the first Law of Love.

🖤 4, 5, 6, 7, or 8, pay special attention to PRIORITY, the second Law of Love.

🖤 9, 10, 11, 12, 13, or 14, pay special attention to EMOTIONAL INTEGRITY, the third Law of Love.

- 15, 16, or 17, pay special attention to DEEP LISTEN-ING, the fourth Law of Love.

- 18, 19, 20, or 21, pay special attention to EQUALI-TY, the fifth Law of Love.

- 22, 23, 24, 25, 26, or 27, pay special attention to PEACEMAKING, the sixth Law of Love.

- 28, 29, 30, 31, 32, or 33, pay special attention to SELF-LOVE, the seventh Law of Love.

- 34 or 35, pay special attention to MISSION IN LIFE, the eighth Law of Love.

- 36, 37, or 38, pay special attention to WALKING, the ninth Law of Love.

- 39 or 40, pay special attention to HELP, the tenth Law of Love.

WHEN TWO PEOPLE CLICK

Chemistry isn't something that can be learned or cultivated. We can't help you force a spark that isn't there, but we *can* help you recognize an ember smoldering so deep beneath the ashes of argument and hostility that it's all but invisible.

If, on assessing the "state of your union," you discovered that your New Couple sum was low in the chemistry department, this chapter will help you understand what that means; and if you conclude that chemistry is present but dormant, the subsequent nine Natural Laws of Love will help you revive it.

So what's this all about? When two people click—when something meshes and there's an instantaneous fit—it's called *chemistry*. This nonscientific use of the term captures the essence of many of our culture's favorite descriptions of love: the attraction of opposites, the recognition of soulmates, love at first sight, even the sense of a long-overdue homecoming. Chemistry is a naturally occurring wonder, an undeniable, powerful force between human beings, and one that continually intrigues and seduces us with its romantic promise. Yet it remains a bona fide mystery to science— one that biologists and psychologists have worked hard to crack. The first Natural Law of Love, the Law of Chemistry, legitimizes this amazing phenomenon: it raises the profile of chemistry, establishing it as a prerequisite for the healthy selection of a mate.

Though chemistry and the intoxication stage of relationship (discussed in the Introduction) are often confused, the two are clearly distinct. The latter is ephemeral—just a phase—characterized by a high that's the result of the excitement of a new connection. Chemistry, on the other hand—though it may or may not be experienced as a high—is a soulful, energetic resonance between two people *which need never dissipate*. This durability is precisely what lends chemistry the solidity to function as the cornerstone of the Ten Natural Laws of Love.

Chemistry is the foundation of rapport; all the other principles of partnership are layered on top of it. This doesn't mean that chemistry never wavers in a healthy relationship. It's predictable—almost inevitable, even—that the chemical magic will weaken as the power struggle intensifies. Luckily, there's an antidote to such chemical entropy—namely, a couple's commitment to the nine other Natural Laws of Love. These have been designed precisely to help keep chemistry alive, especially as couples work their way through the power struggle and move into co-creativity.

It's important to note that the antidote found in the Natural Laws of Love works only if there's something to revive. We can't skip the chemistry altogether, nor should we downplay its importance. Though we like to think that love conquers all, and that good communication or a crackerjack couple counselor can fix all relationships, this simply isn't so. Even the most conscientious application of the nine other Natural Laws of Love can't make up for a serious deficit in the chemistry department.

Having It All—Great Sex *and* Best Friendship

New Couple chemistry has a definition all its own. First of all, lest there be any confusion on this point, it definitely includes great sex. But it goes way beyond a special sexual connection. Two people jell all over the place: their bodies, their personalities, their minds, their hearts, their energies. Bottom line: they're each other's greatest companion by far, in and out of bed, and they acknowledge that both aspects of the relationship are equally important.

This unique form of commingling is more than energetic; it's *synergetic*. Endowing a partnership with a combined level of energy—and therefore potential—that far exceeds what each partner would be capable of alone, it can be both empowering and deeply healing.

Sexual Chemistry: Nectar of the Gods

When sexual chemistry blesses lovers, time and thought cease to exist and the physical form takes on a new essence. Indeed, true lovers often have the impression that their bodies love each other quite apart from their minds (and possibly even their hearts).

While the sex act itself (which drives the perpetuation of the human species) can be quite mundane, sexual chemistry is a matter of the sublime. But beware: relationships afire with sexual chemistry alone are often fraught with drama. Furthermore, because rampaging sexual chemistry can annihilate discernment, the newly initiated can easily get burned. The greatest risk is seen during the early intoxication stage of a relationship, when an intense carnal connection can render new sex partners blind to the reality of the personality they're in bed with. Once the urgency of that connection has faded, they may discover that their relationship has no out-of-bed potential at all; it was just a fling.

It's a worn-out truth in our day that sexual chemistry can impair judgment. It can also be the basis for serial monogamy, a pattern of hopping out of one relationship and into another. The exiting occurs predictably, during that crucial passage out of the intoxication stage into the power struggle, when sexual chemistry starts to fade. We once overheard two twenty-year-old guys, members of a rock band, deliberating over precisely this subject in an outdoor café. "I usually pick girls for sexual reasons," one revealed to his cohort. "But when that intensity starts to mellow, there'd better be something else there." His youthful wisdom was spot on: as we noted earlier, sexual chemistry alone can't sustain any relationship.

Though the shadows cast by sexual chemistry can be long and dark, what can deceive can also inspire. The great trickster named sexual chemistry moves some humans to their highest creative expression. For others of us, sex with chemistry might be the closest thing to a religious experience we'll ever know. And if we desire a long and healthy relationship in the third millennium, delicious sex remains—in tandem with best-friendship chemistry—plainly sine qua non.

Best-Friendship Chemistry

Best-friendship chemistry is rare, and when it occurs it's uncanny. A rapport that's mutually energizing, it makes us feel part of an amazing reciprocal flow.

The recognition of this energetic connection between oneself and another can feel like an unexpected reunion. Both partners are struck with a deep sense of familiarity, of *déjà vu*; it's as though somehow each already knows (and is known by) the other. The blessing of best-friendship chemistry allows two people to deeply "get"—that is, easily and naturally understand, and feel understood by—the other. It makes them curious about and respectful of each other's feelings and opinions. It fosters a genuine mutual admiration that they speak of openly and frequently. It motivates them to stick up for and give one another the benefit of the doubt.

Most important, it allows them to express and hear the truth about what each is thinking and feeling.

Lovers blessed with best-friend chemistry are excited by each other's dreams of the future and laugh at the same things. They delight in each other's company and conversation, though they do just fine apart. Even after years together, they can turn tedium—even something as ordinary as a trip to the recycling center!—into a major adventure. When two people resonate at the same frequency, it doesn't matter what they do. It's fun simply because they're together. Best-friendship chemistry is certainly the most bonding and fulfilling of all interpersonal experiences. In fact, being close this way is what we all crave most.

So does that mean that only partners who have similar personalities can experience best-friendship chemistry? What about the old adage that opposites attract? Unfortunately, there's no hard-and-fast formula for calculating the potential affinity of two personalities. Best-friendship chemistry is a question of partners' energies complementing each other. While that chemistry often expresses itself in similar personalities, it can also show up between so-called opposites.

Though closely interwoven, best-friendship chemistry and best friendship itself are two different things. The latter takes time to develop, while best-friendship chemistry can be experienced instantaneously. This is not to say that two individuals become best friends right off the bat; rather, they feel immediately, in their heart and gut, the potential of best friendship.

At the heart of any best friendship is an essential quality called *emotional trustworthiness*. When two people click, they know in their heart of hearts that the other would never lie to them or intentionally hurt them. Perceiving their relationship as an *emotional safe zone*, they're free to be their authentic selves with each other; and this safety encourages even greater authenticity. In fact, if there's anyone to whom they could reveal all their warts and weirdnesses, their deepest, darkest secrets—not to mention their dreams and general magnificence—it's their beloved other. And he or she feels the same trust in return. At its best, it's an active type of support—one that involves validating, even defending, each other's emotions, thoughts, intuition, and personal rights.

Some people are naturally emotionally trustworthy; others just appear to be. In fact, accurately determining whether a woman we're getting to know really is a "good person" or our new colleague really is a "nice guy" can be an education in itself. Most of us have at least the latent ability to become emotionally trustworthy. But, like any ability, it needs to be developed. Upcoming Natural Laws of Love, including emotional integrity, deep listening, peacemaking, priority, self-love, walking, and help, will provide all the support we need to develop this all-important quality.

Essential Compatibilities—More Is Better

Certainly, it's clear by now why strong and natural best friendship and sexual rapport constitute the basics of New Couple chemistry. But for more and more of us, they aren't enough. Some people see shared dreams, passions, and life goals as equally fundamental to a successful partnership. Others insist that the beloved be of similar intellectual or spiritual bent or possess a simpatico worldview (be it political, religious, or cultural). Still others find creative and artistic kinship to be an essential element in a mate; and there are those who demand that recreational, avocational, or lifestyle tastes be in harmony.

While each of these could actually be considered a kind of chemistry in its own right (depending on the intensity of the energy), they're all, at a minimum, important forms of compatibility. The New Couple model calls them *essential compatibilities*. Unlike attributes, which are characteristics a person possesses—for example, looks, status, money, and education—essential compatibilities involve an orientation to life that can be shared.

It's up to each individual to judge just how *essential* essential compatibilities are. They don't carry the same weight for everybody: one couple might be able to thrive without sharing a particular passion or an interest in philosophy, religion, or intellectual or artistic pursuits, while another couldn't. In some cases, New Couple chemistry is the only long-term elixir needed to launch a healthy relationship. When a couple begins their life together with potent chemistry and a devotion to the health of their relationship, they often develop an array of passions new to both of them, creating essential compatibilities that weren't there at the outset.

Caught Without Chemistry

Thanks to the advent of love marriages, partner-picking in Western culture has been based on love for a number of generations, and in Eastern cultures such choices are ever more common. Ostensibly, this great leap forward for Eros freed us from following the often heavy edicts of family, society, culture, and survival needs; finally, we could follow the dictates of our hearts.

That's the ideal anyway. The reality is that many marriages result not from love but from family, cultural, or religious pressures. This is especially true when pregnancy is involved. Even today, when we're less likely than previous generations to be caught by an unplanned pregnancy, we still "settle" in astonishingly high numbers—in other words, we commit to partners with whom we don't vibrate on all the requisite planes. What is it that compels us to do this—to shortchange ourselves in the single most important relationship of our adult lives?

Usually, the more frightened we are about our emotional and material security (not to mention physical survival), the less able we are to think about our higher-order need for intimacy—the kind of deep intimacy that chemistry affords. If children are on the agenda for the future, as they often are, people sometimes settle as a panicked response, wanting to start this endeavor before it's too late. Women, especially, are frightened by the ticking of their biological clocks.

Fear of ending up alone is another incentive for settling; we might harbor deep-seated worries that we can't take care of ourselves, or believe that we have no value unless we're welded to another person. Even discovering our unique identity as individuals can daunt us, in which case marriage might appear the perfect place to hide. Sometimes we dare not stick to our standards—or even set them in the first place—out of sheer cynicism; we simply despair of ever finding a truly kindred spirit and persuade ourselves that the idea is undiluted fantasy. Such a dim view of committed monogamous relationship probably results from witnessing the failure of our role models' relationships, not to mention our own unhealed heartbreaks.

Any combination of these factors—in addition to, or aggravated by, the family, cultural, and religious pressures mentioned earlier, and by the social stigma associated with singledom—can convince a person to commit without chemistry. If you worry that you settled in committing to your current relationship, Chapter 10's discussion of help will direct you to the assistance you need.

The word "settle" implies a conscious lowering of standards. Sometimes, though, we're so confounded by either sexual or best-friendship chemistry that our standards fly out the window. In some couples the sex is so great that one or both partners lose all discernment and convince themselves that they've got best-friendship chemistry as well. The sexual bond can be so intense that it affects people like a drug, inducing both highs and lows. Such intensity can blind a person to emotional (or even physical) abuse and mask the need for other vital connections, such as best-friendship chemistry, essential compatibilities, and (above all) emotional trustworthiness.

While some of us might find ourselves blinded by chemistry of the sexual variety, others accept relationship without this crucial criterion because the friendship connection is so strong. Treasuring true friendship with someone of the opposite sex, they're willing to overlook a lack of sexual connection, hoping that they can will it into existence. But sexual chemistry is a gift: it can't be created through visualization or developed over time if the initial resonance isn't there.

While for some of us the big lesson about chemistry is that we must insist on both kinds in order to have a relationship that really sings, there are cases in which the all-telling thrill is present but, for complex reasons, is hard to detect. Partners who find themselves in such a predicament often realize that their current relationship isn't the first one missing special pizzazz. Often, chemistry has eluded them with all their previous lovers as well. In that case it's likely that an inability to enjoy exciting sex in a loving relationship is a symptom of a deeper problem—for example, unresolved childhood sexual abuse. An untold number of partners and individuals alike continue to suffer unsatisfactory sex lives— and even sexual proclivities that worry and upset them—because of undiagnosed but highly treatable sexual abuse in their past. A large percentage of people with such problems find that the wounding events are beyond conscious recall. This leaves the symptoms alone to bear witness. Until the trauma is resolved, those symptoms linger on, wreaking havoc in their intimate lives and blocking the ecstatic experience of deep emotional and sexual connection with even the most trustworthy, attractive mates.

Just as sexual chemistry can, for some of us, defy detection, so too can we lack that gut-level knowing that this other person is the one, *even though he or she actually is.* That too is typically the result of childhood wounding. If you doubt your capacity to enjoy chemistry with anyone, perhaps unfinished business from the past is clogging your lines. In that case, immerse yourself in the Law of help. With a bit of diving, you might find the special energies that are there for your love, swirling right under the surface.

The tragedy of a lack of chemistry—whether it's due to settling, faulty discernment, or childhood wounding—lies in the inestimable loss not only of our own happiness but also that of the children that issue from a chemistry-challenged union. It's hard enough to preserve chemistry once we discover a person with whom we really have it. Without these vital juices, however, a relationship can't help but desiccate. The real fantasy is not that our true mate exists, but that true love can be sustained without a new model of relationship and a commitment to work at it.

The Victory of Chemistry over Traditional Sexism

Tradition started the war between the sexes, but we're the ones keeping it going today. Too many of the more traditional among us still see lovers and best friends as two different animals—and marriage as a lifetime in a lockup. We hear it in joking comments such as "Women—you can't live with them, and you can't live without them," "You should always pick a man who loves you more than you love him—otherwise, you might end up broke and alone," and "All guys [or all women] are like that"—whatever "that" may be. Even couples who enjoy many shared interests and revel in great sex are incapable of best-friendship chemistry if they nurture biases about the opposite sex, because such biases preclude emotional trust.

Sexism, man-hating, and misogyny are curses passed down through tradition, but they're also *inevitable* by-products of emotional wounding. We define manhood and womanhood by the role models who bring us up, and the unfortunate among us, having learned about love and marriage from emotionally distant or abusive parents, come by their sexist predispositions honestly; the concept of lover-as-best-friend is simply foreign to them. They can meld sexual chemistry with best-friendship chemistry only after a profoundly healing journey. But what a rewarding journey it is. In their own families at least they serve a grand purpose: ending generations of gender warfare.

The good news is that predispositions aren't set in concrete. People can change how they look at themselves, their gender-role expectations, and the art of relating to others. As they learn the value of deep rapport with self, they begin to insist on deep rapport with another—and nothing less. They're willing to wait for that moment of recognition that tells them without a doubt, *This is the one with whom I'm going to spend the rest of my life.* And they're willing to work at making that happen, a process that begins with making sure their chemistry never diminishes.

Ensuring chemistry's continued presence is what the remaining Natural Laws of Love are all about. In fact, all ten laws are interdependent, because while we need a bold model of relationship (such as the Ten Natural Laws of Love) to preserve our chemistry, only chemistry can inspire us to carry out what those laws propose. Chemistry is the force that empowers us to navigate, in good faith, the perils of the power struggle—and ultimately to cruise into co-creativity. Clearly, every ounce of our couple's chemistry is indispensable. And when together we commit to the whole nine yards—that is, the last nine Natural Laws of Love—we can transform our organic chemistry into couple alchemy and our relationship into gold.

THE KEY TO CHEMISTRY

Insisting on a partner with whom you share both sexual passion and best friendship is the key to the first Natural Law of Love.
This means finding a partner who ...
- ❖ Ignites fires of passion
- ❖ Is emotionally trustworthy
- ❖ Shares any essential compatibilities that are necessary to you

2 PRIORITY

MAKE THE HEALTH OF THE
RELATIONSHIP A TOP PRIORITY

Now that you understand the basics of New Couple chemistry, you have the raw materials necessary to create the sort of enduring, loving relationship all people want. Your next task is to embrace the idea that good chemistry need never be lost. Your commitment to the next nine Laws of Love can put you on the path to a lifetime of true togetherness.

The first stepping-stone is the Law of Priority, which is designed to ensure that the special energies of chemistry don't evaporate during the day-to-day march of our lives. As we've seen, sooner or later even the most perfect new partnership is pulled by developmental tides beyond intoxication and into the power-struggle stage of relationship. Though a loving relationship may be deep and strong, disappointments, disillusionments, and discomfort are sure to crop up, either subtly or otherwise. When this happens, most of us respond as if instinctively. Without knowing it ourselves, we start to emotionally withdraw from—and tune out—our beloved other and focus in on something or someone else. These preoccupations seem, for a time, to help. They afford us relief from the pain of our lack of connection and the anxiety caused by problems piling up.

But we need not follow that unconscious urge to withdraw. If we have the strength and the will to defy that urge, we can renew our chemistry and recommit to our beloved. Not that the relationship ever could or should revert to the all-consuming entity that it was during the intoxication stage. Instead, it ought to develop into a strong, loving crucible in which all the other elements of a joyful life can be forged—a place where self-love and mission in life can be nurtured and draughts of emotional intimacy regularly imbibed.

Who or what might be the symbolic illicit lover that steals the thunder from a precious partnership? Anything—a substance, a behavior, an activity, another person—is a potential culprit. The first challenges to the primacy of love relationships are usually jobs, the people with whom we grew up (that is, our family-of-origin), and favored diversions. Eventually, any of these can crowd out the couple. Of course, other, more visible bedevilments can also snap the connection: these include imbalanced, codependent relationships with people outside the couple, as well as alcohol, drugs, or any other compulsion, addiction, obsession, or psychological problem that rules one or both partners. It's a fact—and a tragically common occurrence—that even the most divinely ordained relationships wilt not only in the presence of such notorious chemistry killers as contempt, violence, and sexual betrayal, but also when exposed to the harshness of behaviors that hurt the individual self. When it comes to the need to make the health of the couple a priority, never has it been more appropriate to say, "Two's company, and three—whether that third is a person, a behavior, an interest, an activity, or a substance—is a crowd."

Commitment with a Capital C:

THE WORK OF RELATIONSHIP

The Law of Priority asks us to go beyond the reranking of life's main events, such as job, church, and family; it even demands more than simply committing to our partner in one of the standard senses—that is, consenting to monogamy, cohabitation, or marriage. More significantly—and this is the revolutionary bit—it requires that we agree upon a new model of relationship, that we become what's described in these pages as a New Couple. Together we vow to apply, to the best of our abilities, the Ten Natural Laws of Love—to do, in short, *the work of relationship*. This assumes that whatever one of us considers a couple issue will be honored as such by the other. Obviously, for any couple, this represents a serious commitment of both time and energy.

Often the deprioritization of a relationship comes about quite innocently. A man who's adjusting to a harsh new boss might retreat nightly to the study to unwind with a drink, thinking that he's sparing his partner his complaints; she might likewise withdraw, not wanting to burden her partner with her concerns about her newly widowed mother. Far from being the result of animosity, their mutual retreat is a polite attempt to spare each other their woes. But that doesn't change the outcome: more and more time spent apart. The couple might instead want to experiment with an after-work walk-and-talk—twenty minutes allotted to clearing away the residue from the day and putting the subjects of boss and mother behind them for the day. That would allow them relief from their worries while conserving chemistry and fostering intimacy.

Seeking strategies that prioritize the couple—that is, doing the work of relationship—doesn't just conserve chemistry; it also potentiates synergy.

As systems theorists tell us, the combined potential of a high-functioning dyad is far greater than the simple sum of its two individual parts. But the incredible energy source within a relationship can be tapped only when we make the health of our relationship a top priority. It's high time that all of us become conscious of—and exploit—the amazing potential of the romantic union. Whatever our goal—be it career, family, avocation, or creative venture—it has a greater chance of succeeding if it's grounded on the bedrock of a prioritized relationship.

Individuation:

GROWING INTO TRUE ADULTHOOD

It might come as a surprise to many that scores of wonderful relationships fall apart every day because, to one degree or another, mates haven't yet emotionally "left the nest." The process of really and truly growing up, of be-coming psychological adults vis-à-vis the people we grew up with, is called *individuation*.

Individuation isn't about running away from, rebelling against, or cutting ourselves off from our parents and siblings; it's about no longer being driven by the need for their approval or ruled by the fear of disappointing, hurting, or angering them. Individuation allows us, as equal and healthy adults, to *choose* whether to accept the guidance and advice of those we grew up with, rather than living under their dominion.

Individuation, like all personal development, is a process. *We don't just jump out of a cab and find ourselves psychological adults.* It's a perennial undertaking – and for some of us it's a real ordeal, because our family-of-origin is the most powerful emotional system we'll ever be part of. It simply doesn't occur to some of us that we can negotiate as adult peers with family members. We perpetuate our roles as eldest child, bad boy, dutiful daughter, rescuing sister, baby of the family, responsible grandson, or attentive nephew and end up double-bound—torn between family and spouse—and stuck in an emotional web of guilt, responsibility, and obligation.

No matter how you slice it, *individuation is about setting clear and healthy boundaries with our families.* It requires, first, that we become conscious when we're feeling burdened, disempowered, or disrespected by family members or are acting out of guilt, obliga-

31

tion, or fear. It then demands that we formulate a clear understanding about what we really want from and with family members. Finally, it asks us to lovingly assert our wishes, putting our new understanding into practice.

Illuminating and untying unconscious entanglements with parents, siblings, and other family members allows us to emerge simultaneously into adulthood and selfhood. It sets the stage for a new kind of exchange with our family-of-origin—ideally, an exchange in which we enjoy equal status as peers. Most important, it allows for—indeed, is a prerequisite for—true partnership within the couple.

When it comes to matters of individuation, a mate's powers of observation are invaluable. Mates are often far more objective about our family-of-origin than we are. As we like to tell the couples we work with, fish are the last ones to know they're swimming in water, much less that the water might be polluted! Just as fish in a tainted tank might assume that water everywhere is purple, we might assume that families everywhere function just like ours—that, for instance, everyone yells at each other or barges in on each other in the bathroom, that all fathers drink a six-pack after work, that all married women make an obligatory phone call a day to parents, that all brothers and sisters try to weasel money from their siblings for questionable (or even admirable) ventures, and that all holiday traditions are sacrosanct. The only certainty about questioning such assumptions is that it will engender feelings of guilt and fear of rejection. These feelings must be faced—and ridden out—by anyone who embraces the process of individuation.

One thing is sure about individuation: it won't happen unless we make it happen. Whether individuation involves separating from parents or from siblings and other family members, it's a rite of passage parents probably weren't designed to initiate. Unless our parents came from another planet—someplace where they were taught how to psychologically nudge their offspring out of the nest—the work is up to us. Leaping into adulthood with our parents' consent is the ultimate act of maturity. *Without that consent*, acknowledging and addressing individuation issues can be the toughest task of our adult life.

Within couples, the importance of supporting each other in this process can't be overstated. If individuation problems have already caused acrimony in your couple, it's critical that you address and heal them. Fortunately, the skills you'll be learning as we discuss the next eight Natural Laws of Love will provide all the help you'll need. With those skills, you'll find that flying the coop of your family-of-origin, while sometimes painful, is empowering and bond-strengthening. Surprisingly, it can ultimately prove liberating even for those from whom you've separated.

Individuation requires that you . . .

- ❖ Become conscious when you're feeling burdened, disempowered, or disrespected by family members or are acting out of guilt, obligation, or fear.
- ❖ Formulate a clear understanding about what you really want from and with family members.
- ❖ Lovingly assert your wishes, putting your new understanding into practice.

Addictions and Compulsions

THE PRICE OF PAYING HOMAGE TO THE GOD OF AVOIDANCE

Everything in the addict's (or compulsive's) life is subordinated to the continuance of the addiction (or compulsion) of choice. When one or both partners suffer from any addiction or compulsion, the beloved other always ends up playing second fiddle.

Addictions and compulsions are defined as repeated behaviors that cause harm to one or more of the core areas of adult life—

namely, health, livelihood, *and primary relationships.* Addicts and those suffering from compulsivity may or may not be aware of either the behaviors or the harm they cause. But even when they are aware, all their attempts at control fail. This out-of-control quality—a blending of powerlessness and self-destructiveness—is the essence of addiction. *It's despair made manifest.* Eventually, both addiction and compulsion render life unmanageable. In intimate relationships, they ruthlessly inhale chemistry and vaporize trust.

It's helpful to separate addictions into two major types, *substance* and *process.* Substance addictions involve something consumable, such as alcohol, drugs, or food. Process addictions, on the other hand, involve activities rather than substances; the major process addictions are work, sex, and gambling. Although it's possible to ruin our lives and relationships overdoing anything, including working out, spending money, watching television, using the computer, playing video games, caregiving, and being absorbed in activity in general, these are usually considered compulsions—lesser beasts—rather than true process addictions. Again, the litmus test for all these is self-destructiveness—that is, a negative impact on health, livelihood, and/or primary relationships—in combination with a lack of control.

When we stay in a relationship with a nonrecovering addict, an untreated mentally ill person, or a criminal—neglecting our own wishes and needs—we fall into the classification of codependents or enablers. We literally *enable* our partner to continue the process of self-destruction, simply by our willingness to maintain a relationship despite his or her behavior. Surprisingly, our denial about the seriousness of the problem can be even more vehement than that of the so-called sick person. Both denials are often fatal to love and always inimical to recovery. Our "support" prevents addicts from hitting bottom—that point at which, finally, the addiction or compulsion causes more problems or pain than it helps avoid. Hitting bottom is a necessary first step in any genuine recovery process.

Truth be told, we're all compulsive about certain things, a little nuts about others. It's only a matter of degree. People with addictions can be warm, loving, generous, and charming. More often than not—some addiction experts say there's a definite correlation—addictive personalities are highly creative and often spiritually inclined. But like the temporary high of a chemical substance, their condition—as long as they're still unrecovered—renders them incapable of sustaining chemistry of any sort, even with work. This is because their primary relationship is to the substance or process that holds them in its grip.

In terms of priority, nothing threatens a couple like the inferno of untreated addiction, mental illness, criminality, and codependence. The drama these disorders engender is pervasive in couples and lies at the heart of much of our work with them. Unless both parties commit to a professional or Twelve-Step group recovery program, couples born in addiction are doomed. The good news is that we've worked with many couples in recovery who've succeeded. In time, many of them have transformed themselves and their relationship, reemerging into some of our most stellar New Couples.

The newest kids on the recovery block—addictions to sex and love—assume many faces. Though the more far-out forms—embellished with all sorts of other kinks—have been amply hyped on television talk shows, the unsensational, often subtle (yet inevitably unraveling) effects of these addictions on true love aren't discussed nearly enough. In fact, many couples routinely tolerate, ignore, or dismiss as inconsequential the manifestations of these disorders.

There's a lot of misinformation and mythology surrounding both sex and love addictions. The first category, sex addiction, isn't the exclusive domain of the clichéd "sex maniac" or "nympho"—the one who seems to want to "do it" all the time with anything that walks. Sex addiction covers a wide range of behaviors and preoccupations of a sexual nature. Some sex addictions are deviant, such as the behavior of pedophiles and your garden-variety flasher in a raincoat; some are not, such as the desire to have oral sex four times a day. Some sex addictions are acted out, such as that of the man who actually has oral sex four times a day, every day; and some are not, such as that of the woman who merely fantasizes about sexual acts in the boardroom with her assistant. Like all addictions, sex addictions are out of control, whether the sufferer admits it or not. Partners thus afflicted aren't bad people; rather, they're symptomatic and need treatment. Almost invariably, they themselves were victimized as children in ways that their present idiosyncrasies echo, although the memories might not be accessible to them.

The second category, love addiction, is a two-headed beast. One aspect hooks people on romance; the other, on relationship. Hardly the realm of the hopeless romantic, there's nothing sweet or cute about all-consuming preoccupations that preclude real feeling. A typical romance addict compulsively seeks that ecstatic, sentimental moment—be it the candle-lit dinner or dancing in the moonlight. While this might seem merely corny—not the stuff of true disorder—romance addiction is no Camelot; it's an emotional disorder with real costs. Romance addicts' first cousins, those who get high on a relationship, commonly feed on the thrill of the intoxication stage of coupledom and fly from person to person in this quest. One well-known form of this disorder is serial monogamy.

Whatever the form of addiction, it flourishes in a climate of silence and/or lies. The codependent partner plays dumb for weeks or months or years, first fostering and then accepting the pretense that all is as it should be. Yet even if not a word is said about such "minor enjoyments" as pornography or cocaine, they're not without consequence. They put hairline cracks in the most precious part of our intimate relationship: emotional trust. The sooner we can all be honest about such issues, the better.

So why do we intimates lie to ourselves? Why do we ignore or pardon behaviors by our partners that, on a deep level, really hurt us? How could we let "minor indiscretions" slide—sometimes until it's too late? Maybe it's because we want to be "cool" about the subject of, say, drugs or sex. In an attempt not to appear petty, puritanical, uptight, controlling, or jealous, we allow a benign tolerance to take hold; we minimize how we feel about these "little" issues, even when they devastate us. Or maybe it's because we tend to sweep things under the carpet generally, in which case we'll surely sequester in the cellar of our unconscious every harbinger of something as heavy as an addiction. And yet addictions are even more likely to spell curtains for the relationship when the acting-out persons—both the addict and the codependent—refuse to admit that there's a problem and commit to recovery.

Confronting addiction is always frightening, especially for the addict. As whistleblowers, we must meet our spouse's initial paralysis and denial in the face of an addiction with the greatest compassion. And we must confront the addiction as a team, calling on that potent synergy that united coupledom engenders.

The Shadow Side of Work

While for almost any couple the need to earn a living is inescapable—and pursuit of a mission in life is always a worthy goal—work can take on the proportions of an addiction or compulsion if prioritized over the relationship. In fact, workaholism, along with derivatives such as type-A behavior, hurry sickness, perfectionism, and compulsive activity, has become a massive problem in our society today.

Ironically, workaholism often generates societal kudos; big business, politics, the arts, and entrepreneurship thrive on it. Indeed, success in some professions and organizations demands a workaholic commitment. Yet nothing drains the life out of a relationship faster than the routine of a twenty-four-hour beeper and a sixty-hour work week. Showing dedication to your job is terrific, but there's a difference between working hard and letting work rule your life. Opting for the latter serves a purpose: for many of us who live this imbalanced lifestyle, it's a grand avoidance. Like any addiction, it functions as an escape from our personal demons and from intimacy. As an issue of priority, it annihilates love.

When a couple struggles with matters of work addiction, both partners typically have underlying issues that need to be addressed. The codependent partner, for example, may be unable to express her needs without being overwhelmed by guilt and thus says nothing as the relationship dies, while the workaholic may see the world only in black-and-white, all-or-nothing terms and thus is unable to conceptualize moderate solutions. The workaholism can't be effectively dispatched until those underlying issues are addressed.

Maintaining Priority in Face of Traditional Pressures

Putting the couple on the back burner has traditionally been seen as both a necessity and a virtue. For our great-grandparents, grandparents, and parents, material well-being, procreation, and childrearing were undeniably the first orders of business.

Sacrificing oneself for one's children, taking care of one's parents, and providing the best possible life one could for those near and dear were cultural norms, and those norms may well have suited the times.

Nonetheless, the effect of those norms on the intimacy and health of couples was debilitating, because the values underlying the norms forced partners to subordinate their own nascent higher-order needs—for self-love, mission in life, and (most relevant to the Law of Priority) true emotional intimacy. Furthermore, people had no formula, no solid model such as the Ten Natural Laws of Love, to assist them in maintaining their chemistry.

The result? Even though in their hearts most traditional spouses deeply cared for each other, their love life was devalued, fading as quickly as a sweet dream—and was replaced by just about everything else. To make matters worse, relationship work simply wasn't done, the subject of love wasn't studied, and there were no relationship experts. As a subject of assessment or improvement, love just didn't exist.

Let's look at two traditional perspectives that continue to haunt couples today.

The Child-Centered Family

"The children must come first" was the credo of yesterday, when any couple who took a holiday without the children caused raised eyebrows at the least and was judged to be negligent at the worst.

And so, in many quarters, it still goes. The traditional belief in the superiority of the child-centered over the couple-centered family is one of the gravest misconceptions we come across as marriage and family counselors.

While it's true that neglect is ever rampant, and that even when material support is ample many kids don't get enough quality one-on-one and family time (especially with fathers, despite the increasing presence of "new dads"), couple-centeredness doesn't mean child neglect. At issue here is many couples' tendency to throw the spouse out with the baby's bathwater. In a hundred and one subtle and unnecessary ways, we're still deprioritizing couple intimacy "for the sake of the children," and that spells danger.

Failure to take care of one's own partnership inevitably results in unmet emotional needs. Some parents unconsciously address those needs by substituting intimacy with their offspring for intimacy with their spouse. This is unfair and hurtful to everyone. It makes the children feel responsible for the troubled parent's emotional welfare, and it allows the troubled parent to ignore the lack of couple intimacy in a way that partners often experience as betrayal.

Another sign that a couple isn't addressing their own emotion-

39

al needs is giving too much "power" to the kids. For example, some parents routinely allow their children to interrupt conversations or sleep with them at night. Others never lock the bedroom door or take time away together. Still others are almost pathologically conscientious in their desire to be available to their children—generally in an effort to avoid their partners or themselves or to compensate for their own neglectful childhood.

In the long term, the price of using children to address adult needs is always the emotional disconnection of the couple, not to mention their sex lives. Some people willingly pay that price, claiming that they'd do anything to help their children. And yet we all know that kids learn more from what parents do—and are—than from what they say. A commitment to paying needed attention to the couple is one of the greatest gifts parents can give their kids: for when the king and queen are sitting squarely on their thrones, children are free to be children, safe in the knowledge that all's well in the kingdom.

The Lopsided Priority: Relationship Work as Women's Work

It could be argued that prioritization of the relationship isn't a new idea at all, that even traditional couples practiced it. Well, sort of. Running the relationship was considered the female domain, since it was generally believed that women were "better at that sort of thing"—an arrangement that freed the male to win the bread and tend to worldly matters. This perspective, which we call the *lopsided priority*, was questionable at best.

What were women tending to anyway, when they ran the relationship? Social life? Church groups and PTA? Their husband's physical health? Real relational health—namely, intimacy, communication, and trust—couldn't have been handled alone by even the most zealous traditional wife, even had it not been terra incognita. Couple health never was and never will be a unilateral affair.

True priority demands that both parties have equal and primary commitment to the health of the couple. Mutuality is paramount.

When one partner (generally the woman) counts on and works toward the centrality of the relationship and the other doesn't, the so-called committed one suffers tremendously. The imbalance shoves the woman into the vulnerable "pursuer" role while the man plays the safe "distancer." She's automatically in the one-down position. This diminishes her self-esteem, and the resulting inequality dashes any possibility for true emotional intimacy.

And yet in many families and across many cultures, women's chronic neglect of self—a kind of martyrdom—has been intentionally role-modeled and elevated to a virtue. Motivated by fears of being alone and discovering their true identity, traditional women over the centuries have been unable to imagine life without the cover of their husbands. And this sad syndrome persists today, as even financially solvent career women fall anew into the trap of lopsided prioritization (or struggle to extricate themselves from it). Panic and desperation—simultaneously causes and by-products of lopsided prioritization—are a heartbreakingly low-grade fuel upon which to run a marriage. Still, run it they do, at great cost.

Occasionally, though not often, the lopsidedness of prioritization tips the other way: the husband is the one devoted to keeping the relationship going. Such a husband is typically the father of children whose mother is sick, emotionally disturbed, or addicted. In the role of ersatz relationship monitor, he's charged with the pragmatics of managing the household as well as seeing to the health of all its relationships; in short, his job is keeping the family together. Even in dismal situations such as this, professional counseling can help both partners prioritize the couple relationship and ensure its greater health, and it can help the "healthy" partner learn how to honor his own limits (and walk if need be).

The New "Mixed" Marriage

As we all know, people today who would be attracted to the New Couple Model don't always end up together; sometimes a potential New Couple partner is married to a traditional. Whether the partners are formally hitched or not, we call such unions "New Mixed Marriage." There are two kinds of such unions. The first starts out with two traditionals; then, somewhere down the road, one partner gets hooked on the subject of higher-order needs and the other partner doesn't. In the second, a man or woman, usually seduced by great chemistries, essential compatibilities or attributes, doesn't make personal development a core condition for a new relationship.

In either case, it usually takes special circumstances (read: *crises*) to catalyze a person into a genuine interest in self-love, mission in life, and emotional intimacy. Triggering events often include death of a loved one, illness, heartbreak, or a perceived failure. Though it may be difficult to see at the time, these losses contain the potential not only to launch us onto a path of self-discovery, but to hatch a New Couple as well.

Envisioning the Ideal

Couples committed to the second Natural Law of Love know that keeping chemistry healthy and vibrant means prioritizing their relationship. They block out time together and pay attention to matters of individuation—taking an honest look at family ties and roles and evaluating how these might be influencing their couple. Equally important, these lovers are on the watch for outside relationships with friends and colleagues that might verge into codependence. They watch their attitude toward work, not to mention their use of alcohol, drugs, food, television, the computer, and anything else that might threaten to control them. Finally, those committed to a more evolved coupledom agree to do the work of relationship with the help of a new model of love. Having sipped from the spring of true chemistry, they are willing to work for long-term emotional intimacy when the beauty and magic start to wane, working out ways to ensure private time together and valuing the joys of an active sex life. They are a testament to the central teaching of the second Natural Law of Love: that is, if the presence of chemistry in a relationship isn't an act of will, its *maintenance* surely is—and first of all, we must prioritize it.

Committing to the second Natural Law of Love and prioritizing relationship isn't an act of heresy; nor, even for people with children, is it selfish. As New Couples can attest, investing time and energy in preserving their God-given chemistry amidst the circus of their lives benefits not just their primary relationship, but also themselves as individuals, their children, their extended family, and even society at large.

THE KEY TO PRIORITY

Prioritizing your relationship to keep chemistry alive is the key to the second Natural Law of Love. This means committing to ...

- ❖ The Ten Natural Laws of Love, which embody the "work of relationship"
- ❖ The process of individuation from your family-of-origin—that is, becoming the emotional peer of parents, siblings, and other extended family members
- ❖ Managing work hours, outside codependent relationships, compulsive behaviors, and the use of food and addictive substances

---

3

EMOTIONAL INTEGRITY

Emotions rule: it's now an established fact. But we can take emotional intelligence to still another level—that of integrity.

Indeed, in his best-seller *Emotional Intelligence*, Dr. Daniel Goleman (writing from a brain-science perspective) concludes that high "EQ"—our emotional sum—vies with high IQ as the heart and soul of human success and fulfillment. This third Natural Law of Love concerns itself with responsibility and wholeness *with regard to our emotions*. It asks us, as partners, to take full responsibility for the whole range of our emotional being. That means we must commit to learning how to deal with the rocket fuel—variously named anger, sadness, fear, guilt, shame, joy, and love—that courses through our bodies, our lives, and especially our intimate relationships. Equally important, we must both agree to examine, on an ongoing basis, the feelings that underlie our behaviors.

This law acknowledges a dangerously neglected fact of committed monogamous life: that the greatest extremes of emotion we're likely to experience in adulthood will come about not only in the crucible of our relationship, but as a result of our being together—especially during the power struggle, the second stage of our couple journey. And the Law of Emotional Integrity provides us with a solution to this problem: real preparedness for the stormy weather that's sure to come. It helps keep emotional explosions—and implosions—from destroying a couple's chemistry, and (as a result) functions as a cornerstone of couple trust.

Specifically, the third Natural Law of Love invites us to commit to being *emotionally honest* with ourselves and each other, and to acquire two essential emotional skills: *emotional literacy* and *emotional management*. Let's look at these three elements more closely:

- EMOTIONAL LITERACY involves both *awareness* (knowing what we're feeling) and *fluency* (being able to speak to each other in the true language of the heart). This aspect of emotional integrity must be addressed first (in life as well as on paper), because without it, neither emotional honesty nor emotional management is possible.

- EMOTIONAL HONESTY means being willing to acknowledge emotional issues and the entire range of our feelings—be they good, bad, or ugly—to ourselves and to our partner. Both honesty and literacy must be in place before emotional management can kick in.

- EMOTIONAL MANAGEMENT requires the willingness and ability to deal with excessive negative feelings proactively, in a healing and creative way.

When a couple commits to the full curriculum—literacy, honesty, and management—they're on the road to emotional mastery in the most modern sense of the term. What's more, they're paving the way to achieving the higher-order needs for love of self and emotional intimacy. (Unfortunately, this curriculum is incomprehensible to those who are unskilled as emotional listeners. That's why deep listening is the subject of the next chapter!)

The Emotional Safe Zone

Emotional integrity is momentous for coupledom, because it exposes an issue that's plagued relationships since people first cohabitated in caves: emotional safety. Whereas love, honor, respect, and the unacceptability of violence have long been the standards of a good marriage, baseline emotional safety has yet to be officially acknowledged as an ideal. An emotionally safe relationship is one in which the healthy expression of each partner's full range of feelings is not only encouraged, but is held to be essential to the longevity of love. This kind of safety necessitates a commitment from both partners that any form of shaming, manipulation, or scaring of the other is unacceptable—and that both partners will do whatever it takes to recognize and weed out such bedevilments.

This law doesn't ask for perfection, recognizing that the willingness to stumble and fall eventually produces the most graceful stride. But it does ask partners to take responsibility for adequate preparation. Like a storm-preparedness protocol, emotional integrity allows us to rest assured that we're ready for most meteorological irregularities.

Literally "energy in motion," e-motions are like the weather. They come and they go, apparently as they please. And whether their waves of energy thrash as forcefully as a gale or undulate as softly as a summer breeze, emotions are a force to contend with. The key to emotional safety is know-how in the form of literacy, honesty, and management. Neither blithe dismissal nor muscling into submission can ever take care of strong feelings. We can no more will our feelings away than shout down the sun. Nor, despite the most valiant efforts, can we tidily stuff them away somewhere. It's a law of physics that energy can be neither created nor destroyed; it merely changes form. So out will our feelings come, in one form or another.

As indestructible—and damaging—as they may be, feelings

have no IQ. Whether welcome or dreaded, rational or apparently irrational, feelings just are; there are no smart or stupid ones. Likewise, the affective realm possesses no inherent morality; in other words, there are no good or bad, right or wrong feelings, either. Still, like other potentially destructive forms of energy, emotions do present ethical considerations, and for that reason they demand some serious responsibility-taking in any couple relationship.

So how should that responsibility be delegated within the couple? Well, ultimately each partner is responsible individually; everyone has a unique emotional weather system for which he or she is solely responsible. But, you may ask, can't a lover make you feel certain ways? Actually, no. He or she might become adept at predicting your reactions and moods, and intentionally push your "buttons" in order to either delight or abuse you. At the end of the day, however, your emotional wiring is your own business—and it's up to you to safeguard it.

Emotional Trauma

THE GREATEST CHALLENGE TO EMOTIONAL INTEGRITY

You'd think that with all the EQ hoopla in the media these days, lovers would have already jumped onto the emotional-intelligence bandwagon and covered half the distance to emotional integrity. Not so. Despite the shelf upon shelf of self-help books designed to bring couples up to emotional snuff, relatively few of us have actually achieved such mastery.

The affective domain is daunting, feelings are confounding—and the reason goes way beyond shyness, pride, character defects, personal communication styles, and gender: most of us, whether we're avid about or disinterested in the subject of emotion, have trouble dealing effectively with our feelings because of a specific kind of emotional wounding called trauma. Usually unidentified, and therefore unhealed, emotional trauma makes dealing with all strong and negative feelings either off-putting or overwhelming for a large share of the population. Many psychologists believe that some kind of emotional trauma (whether major or minor) is at the root of all our neuroses, obsessions, addictions, codependencies, and irksome personality patterns. As if that weren't bad enough, it also keeps bumping us into a fight-or-flight mindset: whenever it rears its ugly head, we fear that we're at risk for not being able to meet our lower-order needs (even though we might have, for example, material abundance, a partner, and family and friends who care about us).

While most people accept the idea that everybody's got "buttons"—highly emotionally charged hurts from childhood waiting to be triggered—it's not so widely known that many of these hurts were actually *traumatic*. In other words, the initial damaging incident wasn't just hurtful to the developing personality, it was shocking. The young self sought emotional protection by going into a daze—that is, psychologically leaving the scene. (This reaction, technically known as *dissociation*, typically looks to the bystander like no reaction at all.) Years or even decades later, when an incident reminiscent of the initial trauma occurs with a partner (or parent or friend), the button gets pushed. The adult self is likely to go back at that moment into some level of shock, repeating the initial daze response. This reaction is often followed by confusion, general upset, even inexplicable rage. The important point for couples is that this sort of innocent replay creates tremendous strife—*and it happens all the time.*

Take, for example, a woman who made a snide remark about her husband's loud shirt as they left for work one day. At first a bit stunned and embarrassed, then perplexed and finally annoyed, the man fumed to himself as they drove to work. Though the woman's remarks, like all judgments, were unacceptable (a form of inappropriately expressed anger, as we'll see later in the chapter), her husband's reaction was also unacceptable—overblown, given the prompt. But he wasn't really reacting to his wife: because he had been harassed as a child by the neighborhood bullies about his parochial-school uniform, he heard that wounding and frightening childhood criticism in her unsolicited comment.

Reactions such as this man's—symptoms of unhealed emotional trauma—are often labeled by the partners involved as either *oversensitivity* or *overreactivity*. The former judges one's feelings to be inappropriate, while the latter focuses on one's actions; but neither is an accurate label. Responses that we categorize as oversensitive or overreactive only seem inappropriate or irrational. While in their current context they're excessive, they're dependable measures of the severity of the original emotional injury.

Whereas for some mates, the trauma theory might seem a little heavy, even implausible, traumatic emotional wounding is in fact universal: we all suffer from it to some degree. Contrary to popular belief, it need not be the result of dramatic, newsworthy events. In addition to "small" incidents such as the above-described bullying over clothing, subtle conditions that occur over time—like growing up with a mildly depressed father or an overworked and impatient mother—often get internalized as normal. These can have as traumatic an impact as terrifying episodes, and they produce similar symptoms. Even seemingly idyllic childhoods can be imperceptibly traumatic. Growing up in messy house, for example—one that engendered embarrassment every time the doorbell rang—can result in an apparently excessive intolerance for clutter.

The good news is that most emotional trauma can be healed. Indeed, we need simply recognize each button as it's pushed, and recall how it was created, to declare the battle half-won.

When it comes to emotions, information is power: general knowledge about emotional trauma can mean insight, freedom, and forgiveness. A commitment by any couple to be aware of unhealed emotional trauma contextualizes both our own and our partner's actions and reactions, revealing the deep logic beneath many of the skirmishes and mayhem of the power struggle. It also encourages compassion. When we learn the sad stories that created our partner's buttons, it's far harder to push them!

Emotional Literacy: Heart Talk

Expression is taken to the level of high art when people become emotionally literate. Emotional literacy entails both awareness and fluency, as we noted earlier. When we're emotionally aware, we're able not only to know what we're feeling, but also to differentiate feelings from thoughts. When we're emotionally fluent, we're able to talk about the whole spectrum of our feelings.

Emotional Awareness

Emotional awareness is the innate but often stymied ability to identify whatever feelings are true for us at any given moment. We can't afford to overlook this ability or let it atrophy, because when we're out of touch with our feelings, we're out of touch with our deep desires and our higher-order needs. Fear, for instance, cues us when our personal safety, be it psychological or physical, is at risk; this protective function is a vital aspect of self-love. Excitement and passion, even envy, help point us in the direction of our true work, our mission in life. And the ability to feel compassion is inseparable from authentic friendship, a pillar of emotional intimacy.

It's often said that there are only two feelings, love and fear, and that all others are simply derivatives. While this may well be so, we all need to be familiar with the common short list: joy, relief, anger, sadness, shock, guilt, shame, jealousy, fear, and love. With the exception of special forms of guilt and shame, these are all generally healthy—that is, they serve to preserve and affirm life.

The so-called shadow emotions—namely, toxic types of guilt

and shame, as well as the so-called contempt cluster, which includes hatred, scorn, disdain, and contempt—are neither natural nor healthy, because they're based on false and hurtful assumptions about ourselves and others. Capable of exercising tremendous power over our existence, these ugly emotions are also the cause of untold couple jeopardy. Toxic guilt and toxic shame are both twisted forms of fear, the sad by-products of a distorted sense of who we really are. The contempt cluster, on the other hands, results from anger unexpressed over a long period of time. Not surprisingly, our unhealthy emotions almost always stem from our childhood days and those notorious emotional traumas. (The shadow emotions will be further discussed later in the chapter.)

Whether we know it or not, whenever two people communicate, emotion is not only present, it drives the interaction. Though we'd like to believe that *thinking* is what motivates us, in fact our thinking merely implements the dictates of our emotions. That's why emotional awareness is so crucial. And it's something we all can master.

Fortunately, being emotionally aware isn't an all-or-nothing proposition; none of us is completely out of touch with all of our feelings. All of us who were initially drawn together as couples based on best-friendship chemistry have at least a *pinch* of emotional awareness; otherwise, we couldn't have experienced the trust that made us able to become intimate friends. So it's not gross emotional blindness that's at issue here; it's selective blind spots— a lack of awareness with regard to specific emotions. (The term *blind spot* can also describe an inability to see issues that affect the couple and a lack of insight about what underlies them.)

Everyone has specific emotions that are problematic. These are, as you might guess, largely the fallout of unaddressed childhood emotional trauma. Surprisingly, the expunging of troubling emotions through blind spots plays no favorites: even those feelings assumed to be easiest for couples—namely, appreciation and love—are sometimes relegated to the periphery of consciousness, as are the more expected sadness, fear, guilt, shame, jealousy, and anger. Emotional awareness demands that we pay close attention to our own emotional state and learn to identify what we're feeling.

What Feelings Are and Are Not

One cardinal task of emotional awareness is distinguishing emotions from thoughts. They're two entirely different animals. Thoughts include opinions, ideas, beliefs, judgments, and fantasies, to name just a few; and they're centered in the head. Emotions, many of which we've named in this chapter, are centered in the body. When they're experienced, they're accompanied by a specific group of physical reactions. Fear might begin as a tightening of our chest or stomach area, for example, and crescendo into shaking or trembling. Thoughts, on the other hand, don't themselves trigger physical reactions. However, they commonly trigger emotions, which then produce physical reactions. Imagine, for example, that you're trapped alone in a room with a bear. The idea of being trapped with a bear might provoke the feeling of anxiety (a form of fear), which in turn might cause your pulse to race.

Language contributes to our tendency to confuse feelings with thoughts—and to our emotional illiteracy. Say, for instance, that a husband tells his wife, "I feel that you were wrong to do that." This appears to be an expression of feeling. That's only because he used the word feel, however. The statement would have been more accurate if the man had said, "It's my opinion that you were wrong to do that." Though most opinions, like judgments and ideas, involve underlying emotions, they're part of the thought family and constitute activity of the intellect. Our feelings, on the other hand, are kinesthetic and constitute activity of the heart. Because we can't be truly intimate until we can share our feelings, any couple who mistakes a product of the intellect for a message from the heart is destined for discontent.

Emotional awareness also asks us to assign feelings their correct names. For some of us, this isn't the cakewalk it appears to be. Traditionally, terms such as "bad," "tired," "upset," "bored," and "depressed" have passed for feelings. Not emotions themselves, they're actually a kind of code—face-saving substitutes for the real thing. (Remember, emotional directness has long evoked allergic reactions!)

"Bad" almost always means "sad" or "guilty." "Tired" can be either a bodily or emotional state (or a combination of both); as an emotional state, it's usually a reaction to anxiety or stress, which are members of the fear family. The word "upset" is often used to describe an admixture of anxiety, disappointment, and frustration. "Bored," which we all recognize as a teen favorite, is widely used by adults as well. It connotes denied or numbed feelings—generally a stew of anger, sadness, and fear. Used casually, "depressed" usually means "sad." Depression itself isn't a feeling; rather, it's a serious emotional condition that develops when we numb our emotions over a long period of time.

Emotional Toxins

Guilt and shame, interlopers in all love relationships, aren't generally recognized as having healthy and toxic varieties, but they do. Since we can't be expected to identify, or be aware of, feelings we've never heard about, these tricky emotions wreak considerable havoc in our lives.

Let's look at the healthy/toxic distinction. *Healthy* guilt lets us know when we've hurt someone by, for instance, breaking a promise. Though uncomfortable, this feeling has positive consequences: it discourages a repeat performance and teaches us to be more trustworthy in general. *Healthy guilt always and only results in corrective action.* *Toxic* guilt, on the other hand, grows out of low self-love. It involves an unfair accusation—a guilt-trip we place on ourselves—that persuades us we're responsible for someone else's feelings. For example, we feel guilty when we say no, so we say

53

yes—and then live to regret it. Toxic guilt, the signature symptom of codependence, always has negative consequences: it holds us accountable for the emotional status of others and coerces us into rescuing them. When we succumb to it, we give ourselves away, damage our self-love, and patronize the person we intended to help.

Shame is another two-faced emotion that couples must be able to both identify and nail. *Healthy* shame is reflected in a reasonable, self-protective concern about maintaining the high regard of others. *Toxic* shame, like toxic guilt, is a key characteristic of codependence and low self-love. It results in the unreasonable fear of being suddenly exposed to others as unlovable, inadequate, and rejectable—*even though these beliefs about ourselves are lies.*

The first kind of shame honors us as social animals; it keeps us from behaving in ways that risk ostracism, which few of us have the ego strength to tolerate. It would be self-destructive, for instance, to make love in one's front yard in plain view of the neighbors. Luckily, healthy shame wouldn't allow it. The second, toxic kind of shame, doesn't proscribe certain behaviors; rather, it vilifies the individual from within. Healthy shame calls our action self-destructive; toxic shame condemns us as wrong or bad. Toxic shame makes many of us so concerned about what others think of us that that concern becomes a motivating force in our lives and intimate interactions.

The toxic emotions are so powerful that they completely overshadow healthy emotions. That's why women often have trouble getting in touch with their anger and men typically can't own their sadness and fear. When these feelings are expressed in childhood, boys are humiliated and girls are warned that they're making themselves unlovable. That's how toxic guilt and toxic shame, and their accompanying terror of abandonment, are seeded. In both sexes, the direct and natural expression of gender-proscribed emotions activates the same gut-level fear of being disapproved of—and ultimately abandoned. Here there's no gender gap; we're all afraid of the same thing.

Sometimes, uncannily, an emotion that one partner is unable to recognize or express shows up as an emotional excess in the other. It's as if the sighted partner is trying to supply what the blind partner can't. It's a sort of unconscious emotional lending. One of our stiff-upper-lip male clients, in talking about his wife's copious tears after the death of his father, said, "My wife had to express the grief for both of us." It took scaling a wall of toxic shame for that man to mourn in an emotionally healthy way.

Emotional Fluency

Emotional fluency, the second component of literacy, involves our ability to speak the language of emotions in the most straightforward way possible. This is best accomplished by using I-statements, a formula in which the words "I feel" are followed by whichever emotion is appropriate. (For example, "I feel embarrassed when you interrupt me.") Despite the fact that this old communication workhorse remains the cutting edge for couple communication, it's stunningly underemployed.

Although to the uninitiated the formula of the I-statement might appear contrived, even silly, the I-statement is a lifesaver for couples. Like neurotransmitters for the heart, I-statements enable communicators to travel safely over highly charged material and open new pathways to each other. When properly used, I-statements effectively keep the poetry and drama of human intercourse from becoming volatile or destructive.

Does that mean that these special messengers induce boredom? Not at all. In fact, though few couples realize it, the cause of boredom in relationships is the withholding of emotional truth, not the absence of volatility. Conversely, the sure cure for couple doldrums is a bold session of truth-telling. Because I-statements are designed to facilitate this level of dialogue, they have the power to bring forth lots of passion.

True emotional intimacy is the province of the emotionally fluent—namely, those well versed in the use of I-statements.

Romance would be short-lived indeed if we lovers couldn't identify our warm feelings and articulate to each other those three crucial little words: "I love you." Still, important as affection is, it represents but one stripe of the rich rainbow of emotions we need to express, I-statement style, in order to enjoy this delicious, nonsexual form of intimacy. Technicolor communication is serious business for couples, and the short list of emotions just won't do.

The Full Monte

The "full monte" includes six families of emotion (each with several members) that you'll eventually want included in your repertoire of expression. These groupings are. . .

1. Shock, Surprise, and Confusion,

2. Anger, rage, resentment, frustration, annoyance, irritation, impatience, and the contempt cluster (which we met earlier)—that is, hatred, scorn, disdain, and contempt.

3. Sadness, grief, disappointment, hurt, and despair.

4. Fear, anxiety, worry, insecurity, panic, jealousy, and toxic guilt and shame.

5. Healthy guilt and shame, and embarrassment.

6. Love, joy, admiration, appreciation, gratitude, relief, empathy, and compassion.

Don't let the length of this inventory daunt you. It's likely that these terms are already embedded in your vocabulary. Attaining fluency is mainly a matter of slipping them into I-statements.

While people generally agree that communicating the warm,

fuzzy emotions strengthens any union, many lovemates have difficulty believing that communication of the so-called negative feelings (the ones featured in groupings one through five) could ever prove bonding—even if they're presented as I-statements. This aversion to expressing the pricklier sorts of feelings is understandable, given how little exposure most of us have had to the appropriate form of such expression. Still, it's better to air those prickly feelings in honest conversation—gently, kindly, and using I-statements—than to let them fester.

Emotional Honesty

The concept of emotional honesty, the second dimension of emotional integrity, is a little confusing for some couples. Often it's equated with the generic brand of honesty—the Honesty with a capital H that made George Washington and Abe Lincoln famous. But no, this isn't about divulging trysts and offshore bank accounts (though lying about such details is clearly destructive). Rather, emotional honesty is about our willingness to acknowledge our true feelings—*all* of them – as well as emotional blind spots and issues that affect our partnership. It's honesty in its next incarnation—similar, yet more refined.

If this seems a bit over the top, don't worry. Being willing to do something isn't the same as *doing* it. It would be crazy to point out every single feeling as it strikes us, or to deliver blow-by-blow reports each other on every erotic dream or feeling of attraction that registers. Likewise, emotional honesty isn't a license to abuse our partner with abrasive opinions (which aren't feelings anyway, but thoughts). This special kind of honesty asks only that we acknowledge emotional states if they become problematic for either partner; it demands a commitment to be as *emotionally real* with each other as we possibly can. That's it.

Because it's hard to be real when we're not conscious of our feelings, emotional honesty includes a commitment to become conscious (if we're not) and then tell the truth about what we feel. Honesty also demands that we listen to each other nondefensively and with an open heart. Thus the art of deep listening will be taught in the next chapter.

Emotional honesty is very different from emotional awareness and emotional fluency: whereas awareness entails knowing what we feel, and fluency entails knowing how to speak what we feel, honesty is the willingness to speak what we feel to our mates—and *face whatever blind spots or issues threaten the trust between us.* This is as real as it gets. As you can see, each element of emotional integrity is a prerequisite for the next: we can't honestly speak up if we don't know what's up or how to get it across in an acceptable way.

Blind Spots and Emotional Safety

A mutual commitment to emotional honesty is a giant step toward creating an emotionally safe relationship—especially when we pledge to explore those blind spots. As we've said, practically every thought, word, and deed that transpires between people is driven by emotion. We're in effect bombarding each other with emotional messages and subjecting each other to emotion-driven behavior all the time.

Any emotional benightedness either partner suffers from is a setback for the relationship. Whether it's general resentment and anxiety or disappointment at our mate's reluctance to go to our high school reunion, feelings that we disown end up coming out anyway—by default and willy-nilly. That's why a commitment to illuminate as many blind spots as we can identify is essential not only to the emotional safety of our union but also to our precious chemistry. If we can get those squirrelly feelings and issues into our sights and talk about them, we can catch—and defuse—them before they build up to the level of implosion or explosion.

But busting blind spots is much more than an excellent measure of prevention for couples. In waking ourselves up to our deeper emotional truths, we simultaneously raise our level of self-love. While this dual process helps reveal those areas where we need to heal, it also points toward the direction of our greatest bliss.

Would that we could sit atop mountains, suss out our blind spots, and become completely emotionally honest on our own— before we entered relationships. We'd be spared a lot of work, not to mention the sometimes disconcerting experience of having our partners see our blind spots first. All alone, however, such enlightenment is almost impossible to achieve, and attempting it encourages a state of self-delusion. The semi-solo route—reading self-help books, attending workshops, and going through therapy—is more viable; indeed, one can face many facets of oneself in this way. Still, no matter how we slice it, *the fast track to emotional honesty is always committed relationship.* For when it comes to scoping out blind spots, mates are endowed with night vision. If you commit to emotional honesty—and allow the loving scrutiny of your partner to penetrate your darkest corners—you will be enlightened. Over time, you'll feel your way into who you really are. Such is the agony and ecstasy of emotional honesty and long-term togetherness.

Obstacles to Emotional Honesty

At times all of us in partnerships have trouble being emotionally honest; we're unwilling to acknowledge our true feelings about certain issues—even when our silence threatens the trust between us. When we're aware of the truth but refuse to utter it, or are defensive or dishonest, it's not because we're scoundrels or pathological liars. Our deceit is yet another complicated side effect of unhealed early trauma. Childhood trauma not only creates a host of buttons and blind spots, as we've seen, but it also makes emotional honesty exceedingly difficult. In fact, revealing specific feelings (or facing certain issues) can feel to the unhealed part of a person like a risk to dignity, security, or some other precious commodity—even life. Only when the early trauma is addressed and the healing has begun can emotional honesty grow.

Sexual jealousy is another common obstacle to emotional honesty. It has a long-standing reputation as the shadow side of love. And because it's shameful in our society to be needy or insecure, sexual jealousy is shrouded in toxic shame. Hence jealousy is particularly hard for us to be honest about. Complex and powerful, it's perhaps unparalleled in its capacity to destroy trust and intimacy.

Despite—or perhaps because of—its importance, sexual jealousy is often misunderstood. Though it's commonly associated with humiliation, revenge, and withdrawal, these are but the jagged edges of the emotion expressed indirectly; they're not jealousy itself. Like Beauty's Beast, sexual jealousy gets banished from consciousness and then gets really ugly.

Sexual jealousy is a bitter cocktail of both toxic shame and abandonment panic, which has its roots in abandonment trauma. The fear of being assessed as less desirable or lovable than somebody else—and then dumped for it—surely makes sexual jealousy the most dangerous emotion we risk feeling when we allow ourselves to fall in love.

Like all emotions, this heavyweight is universal. We all have the potential to feel sexually jealous, even if we haven't had occasion to experience jealousy consciously or have trouble owning up to it. Many of us who feel powerless over our beloved's opinion of us respond with rage. This affords us a temporary (though false) restoration of power and dignity. Others of us respond by denying any feelings of jealousy to ourselves, to our mates, or both. We can end up either withdrawing into a haze of fantasy, intoxicants or other escapes, on the one hand, or seeking revenge on the other.

Being honest about jealousy up front can keep our relationship from going either numb or ballistic. Sometimes, however, being aware of and honest about our feelings of sexual jealousy isn't enough to diminish their intensity; in these instances, emotional management is necessary.

Emotional Management

Emotional management hinges on one absolutely crucial skill: *our ability to distinguish between acting feelings out and expressing them in a healthy way.* Our commitment to learn this vital distinction, and to then refrain from acting out, is at the heart of emotional management. Successful emotional management also depends on emotional literacy and emotional honesty, because we can't deal responsibly with a negative feeling if we're unaware of it, can't articulate it, or aren't willing to tell the truth about it.

Since the only way we can properly manage our anger, grief, fear, jealousy, and toxic emotions *with our partner* is through responsible expression, the only way to healthily communicate about these issues is through I-statements. (Of course, as individuals, we can work to resolve our negative feelings through emotional catharsis as well—through crying, for example, or the kind of anger-release work done in the safety of a therapist's office.) Every other means of feeling-centered communication with our beloved—whether it's body language, facial expression, verbalization, deliberate silence, physical behaviors, or even sighing—is, quite simply, a different variety of acting out.

Consider these examples: Nellie acted out her anger at Owen when she slammed the car door. Quinn acted out his grief over his lost cat when he spent the whole weekend locked in the cellar eating ice cream, watching the old black-and-white television, and ignoring his wife. Tally acted out her anxiety when she nagged Zeb to check the gas range twice before he left the house. Glen acted out his toxic guilt when he looked sheepish and apologized to his girlfriend after she stood him up.

Though the styles in which we can act out our emotions are as limitless as human creativity, they're all hurtful. The reason is simple: acting out always involves a victim. And that unlucky victim will be you, your mate, or (if you have kids) your little ones. As unbearably humdrum as it may seem to ask lovers to stick to such a rigid protocol for informing each other about hard-to-share feelings, only I-statements are honest, effective, and humane.

Anger: Acting It Out and Acting It In

Lots of acting out occurs because we're emotionally illiterate. Like our parents and our parents' parents before them, we innocently conduct our emotional lives according to what we learned in our families. Yet even some of us who've successfully gotten in touch with our feelings, who know about I-statements and are capable of being emotionally frank, still act out occasionally or even frequently.

Why do we persist in acting out? Unaddressed trauma is again the culprit, raising its ignominious head. More often than not, unilluminated blind spots, unhealed buttons, and unresolved issues compel the emotionally unskilled and the skilled alike to act out. The situation becomes exponentially more complicated the longer it continues unaddressed, because by their very acting out, traumatized intimates unwittingly retraumatize each other—and traumatize their children. A terrible couple and family ordeal is inevitable when negative emotions seep, slip, or otherwise emerge without our conscious control.

For couples, anger seems to be the greatest emotional challenge. Like a noble warrior's sword, in its healthy form anger performs a mighty function: it lets us know when our rights are being violated, helps us uphold our self-esteem, and keeps us safe. But in order to receive its gifts, partners must be trained to wield it.

The first task in that training is to *own* anger. If we fail at that task, anger can turn into a veritable monster. If we refuse to allow anger into our awareness, or sequester it uncommunicated, over time it goes bad. If denied its true expression, it has no choice but to deform itself into hatred or contempt, and in that state it's usually displaced onto a target or issue more acceptable to our unconscious. Think of the road-rager who acts out on the freeway, for example. He isn't principally angry at the driver who cut him off

LAW 3: EMOTIONAL INTEGRITY

(though even he probably doesn't know who he is angry at). When anger is deformed into hatred or contempt *within a couple*, the explosion into violence—be it verbal, physical, or emotional—can go one of two ways: either we act out our feelings against ourselves, or we act them out against our partner—either of which can permanently damage trust.

Acted-out anger has long been known to come in two basic varieties: aggressive-aggressive and passive-aggressive. Even today, Freud's clunky jargon provides the best description of the great anger divide, because both types need to be seen as aggression (though passive aggression, being less direct, is sneakier and harder to substantiate). Aggressive-aggressive behavior includes verbal abuse, coercion, threats, throwing and breaking things, and physical violence. Passive-aggressive behavior, on the other hand, includes victim talk, patronization, sarcasm, teasing, denial, withdrawal, and innumerable forms of sabotage.

Like acting out anger, acting it in is the result of our inability to express emotion directly; the difference is that instead of turning angry feelings against our partner, we turn them against ourselves. While we're all familiar with the phenomenon of "beating ourselves up," most of us haven't been taught that self-abusive behaviors, as well as toxic self-talk, are responses to unhealthy guilt and shame. Eventually this kind of emotional mismanagement can lead to compulsions and addictions.

Inciting Anger: You-Statements

Besides versing themselves in the intricacies of passive-aggressive and aggressive-aggressive behaviors, another way modern couples can clean up their anger act is by editing their verbal communication. The weeding out of the you-statement can work miracles of peace and harmony. This evil stepsibling to the healthy I-statement was exposed in all its destructiveness by parenting expert Thomas Gordon. While he proscribed the use of you-statements as abusive to any child at any speed, the list below shows how harmful they can be to lovers too. In fact, you-statements, which have a distinctly authoritarian tone, account for nearly all the verbal acting out of anger between partners.

Let's set the stage for the examples we list below: Lynette was stinging from a recent humiliation by her husband's best friend, Joel. Chet had made no attempt to protect her, nor did he acknowledge the incident later. When she tried to bring it up, he dismissed it as trivial. Lynette was beside herself with feelings of betrayal and sadness but had no idea how to express her concern to him directly. Then, when Chet announced his intention to take Joel for a ride in his new car, she lost it. Here are some examples of the you-statements she might have launched at him, adapted from Gordon's *What Every Parent Should Know* and sorted according to different categories of verbal abuse:

SARCASTIC: I suppose you want to take Joel out to dinner now?

THREATENING: You'll be sorry if you go out with Joel.

SHAMING: Are you going running to Joel again?

ORDERING: You call Joel this minute and tell him you're not coming.

WARNING: If you see Joel, he'll probably insult you too.

INTERROGATING: What were you thinking when you told Joel you'd pick him up?

MORALIZING or PREACHING: You shouldn't fraternize with a person like that, even if he is your best childhood buddy.

ADVISING: I'd stay away from that guy [if I were you].

EVALUATING: Clearly you don't know any better than to go to out with him again.

> PSYCHOANALYZING: You're obviously continuing in your childish pattern of not being able to say no.
>
> TEACHING: You need to learn how to stand up for me with your friend.
>
> GUILT-TRIPPING: If you pick him up after what he did to me, I'm never going to be able to hold my head up again around your friends.
>
> BLAMING: You're trying to humiliate me by going to see him.

Although it may seem anticlimactic, the only healthy and respectful way Lynette could have communicated her anger to Chet is via the simple I-statement: "I'm angry and hurt that you're going out with your friend after he insulted me." Though prosaic, this communication is clean and fair—a good prelude to psychologically mature dialogue between the partners.

Acting Out Fear

While most love partners are all too familiar with the faces of anger acted out or acted in, fear slips by us with little fanfare. Despite its low profile, the fear family—including anxiety, stress, panic, and terror—can seriously destabilize a relationship if acted out. Consider the woman who reminds her husband every single morning not to let the cat out as they leave for the day, or the man who scares his whole family by insisting on keeping a veritable arsenal of semiautomatic weapons in the cellar "just in case."

This sort of interaction occurs in epidemic proportions in couples today. "She's just neurotic" or "He's such a control freak" are typical of the ways we minimize, rationalize, and often dismiss these manifestations of fear. The truth is these behaviors—and an infinite number of others—belong on our ever-growing list of symptoms of unresolved trauma.

Unresolved trauma leads some people to micromanage their

life, because that behavior gives them the impression that they have a modicum of control. Then, when something goes awry— they're blocked, or told no, or presented with a frustrating situation—they blow. But it's not necessary to live with free-floating fears; they're substantially healable, if the underlying trauma can be recognized and addressed.

The Management Alternative

As we've seen, emotions are wildcards; they're not what we'd call controllable. Still, we have a great alternative to acting them out: managing them. Once we learn the simple but priceless distinction between healthy and destructive communication of feelings—in other words, between management and acting out (or in)—we're well on the way toward the goal of emotional integrity. When we then actually practice using I-statements, we come closer still. But the real points are scored when we recognize that all our irritating, out-of-control, and unloving communications, be they expressed in word or in deed, are more than just blind spots, buttons, and unresolved issues. They're the consequences of serious early hurts, and as such they deserve a lot of patience and require a lot of hard work. Such hurts don't heal by themselves.

For most of the feelings people typically act out, including mild anger, the basics of this chapter—emotional literacy, emotional honesty, and emotional management—provide a thorough foundation to help a couple uphold its emotional integrity. If, however, you experience a surfeit of anger (which happens to all of us more frequently than we wish), the anger management and conflict technology of Chapter 6, "Peacemaking," will teach you and your partner exactly what to do.

How Emotional Integrity Transforms Coupledom-

Social convention has always taught spouses to conduct themselves with integrity. *Love, honor, respect* and *cherish* were catchwords of the traditional marriage, and they're still unquestionably fitting ideals for committed relationship today.

The problem for earlier generations lay in the achievement (as it still does for us). How could spouses be expected to live up to these ideals when their emotions—the highly potent fuel of everyday interactions and behaviors (indeed, of their very existence)—remained largely unknown, unexplored, and unmanaged? As we know, many couples fell short. Not knowing what went wrong, they couldn't help but incriminate themselves—or their beloved other.

Instead of worrying about emotional integrity, partners of the past were preoccupied with emotional permission—that is, with what they were and were not allowed to express. For life partners specifically, the socially acceptable emotions were limited to a grand total of one: love. As vital and healthy as the so-called negative emotions are, they weren't so lucky: the less visible they were, the better.

In addition to restricting what people could do with the feelings they had, tradition also dictated who could experience which emotions. Feelings were traditionally distributed along gender lines. In many cultures, both East and West, men have historically been given free rein to experience anger and, on certain occasions, joy. However, as we mentioned earlier, the expression of the "feminine" emotions of fear, sadness, and love has been seen and felt as (toxically) shameful for men. Women, on the other hand, have been able to show love openly, as well as fear and sadness, but anger (perceived as aggressive and therefore unladylike) has been weighed down by societal disapproval. Under such severe pressure, women's anger (obeying the laws of energy) has necessarily shown up dysfunctionally in themselves and in their intimate relationships.

Fortunately, things are changing for the better. As we now know, emotional integrity is about loving, honoring, respecting, encouraging, and validating the full spectrum of our healthy feelings—and those of our beloved other. As revolutionary as it may seem, when we commit to the third Natural Law of Love, we're doing much more than taking responsibility for the power of our own affective world. We are, perhaps for the very first time in the history of romantic relationship, addressing the ideal of emotional safety. Though it's a fact few have been educated to know, all love partners are sitting atop mysterious reservoirs of unexpressed emotions, some of which date back to our earliest days. These murky emotional waters are destined to be brought to the surface when, during the power struggle especially, we inadvertently—yet inevitably—bump into each other's biggest emotional blind spots and buttons.

A couple's sincere and mutual effort to become literate, honest, and adept at managing emotions not only lays the groundwork for peace, an emotional safe zone, and a new kind of relational sanity, it also creates ongoing opportunities for essential purification. For no matter how wild an emotion may be, a known feeling is always easier to tame than an exiled feeling—and a conscientious effort to get in touch with each one of our feelings is worth its weight in gold. Mastering basic emotional management skills, as well as the deceptively simple I-statement, is fundamental to maintaining the emotional integrity of any relationship. And because, as we'll see in Chapter 6, these skills are also the first steps in the resolution of conflict, we might never know how many El Niños even a little such competency has kept safely offshore.

Though it may be a stretch, and will certainly require deep trust in ourselves and our beloved, the willingness to dig out those old buried feelings and face them—even those we'd rather hide from ourselves and everyone else—can transform our lives. And as partners in New Couples frequently notice, the more comfortable we get with our own emotional privates, the more willing we are to allow our beloved a regular peek. (Sometimes, when called for, we might even permit a stranger—in the form of a therapist—to look as well.) And what a relief! Because once we know how to appropriately listen, the simple act of telling each other our emotional truth is the principal way we can clear up those awful, self-punishing feelings of toxic guilt and toxic shame that riddle us all.

The only way, then, is up. With a commitment to this third Natural Law of Love, we'll find that we naturally continue to inspire each other to ever greater heights of awareness, expression, and honesty. Over time, when early hurts are positively identified and empathized with, we might even experience some miraculous healings. Our self-love will shoot up, and we'll experience more space for feelings of fun in our emotionally safe relationship. Telling the truth will never feel the same again!

THE KEY TO EMOTIONAL INTEGRITY

Examining and healing emotional blind spots, buttons, and issues that cause either partner strife and establishing an emotional safe zone is the key to the third Natural Law of Love.

This means learning the skills that enable you to take full responsibility for your emotions—specifically, to. . .

- ❖ Become emotionally literate—that is, aware and fluent
- ❖ Become emotionally honest
- ❖ Manage all feelings, including those that are extreme

THE GREATEST GIFT OF LOVE

Perhaps the divine human design—one mouth, two ears—was intended specifically for couples, a subtle indication of the correct ratio of talking to listening.

It's divine indeed when partners can listen to each other twice as much as we talk. If we choose, we can shift the more passive part of interpersonal relating into an even higher gear—and learn to deeply listen. For while listening is still the greatest gift of love, *deep* listening is the gift that makes love last.

Together with emotional integrity, deep listening—that is, listening from the heart—is the essence of emotional support. It's different from the everyday sort of listening in that it offers no advice or judgment, nor does it attempt to fix anything. The silence it entails opens a delicious space, one that invites our beloved to go really deep, to contact and express the purest forms of his or her feelings, whatever they may be. The fourth Natural Law of Love asks us to listen not just for the story, but for the feelings our partner is having about the story. Deep listening functions, then, as the receptive end of emotional integrity, enabling the listener to field for the speaker the very feelings that emotional integrity helped both partners get in touch with, express, and be honest about. The most exalted form of deep listening empowers us to cull from our partners even their so-called negative feelings *about us*. For when done responsibly, such truth-telling is the surest way to keep lovers from drifting apart.

This modern age, with its aural overload, seems to be all about transmission, not reception. Everyone, including romantic partners, is being turned into a listening target. Assaultive sound bites, coming from all directions and at high volume, are shortening our attention span, causing information indigestion, and numbing lovers emotionally. To keep ourselves from going nuts, we've all had to go a little deaf.

A Crisis of Listening.

You'd think that in this modern-day Babel we'd treasure the simple refuge of each other, eagerly seek the oasis of quiet that our relationship can provide. But this is often not the case. Instead, many of us go home and look for serenity in our audio-enhanced computer gadgetry and televisions. "Quiet" evenings with each other are spent watching videos in surround-sound or otherwise "recovering from the day." Unfortunately, however, when we're plugged in to entertainment, we're typically tuned out from each other.

Recent information technology has created its own unique stresses, contributing to greater societal depersonalization than ever before. Still, the romantic estrangement many of us experience is nothing new. Though far more expensive, the high-tech toys of today function much as the silent newspaper did in our parents' generation: besides helping everyone unwind, these gizmos also serve in part to cloak the emotional alienation that spreads subtly and gradually over lovemates—even partners who started out mad about each other. Clearly, whether we know it or not, what couples need now is (as the old song suggests) love, sweet love, in the form of being listened to—truly, madly, and deeply—every day.

Like emotional awareness, deep listening is a natural human

ability that comes easily to each of us if we let it. So why does it continue to be such a bear for couples? After all, lovers rarely start out unable to listen to each other. During the intoxication stage of relationship, many of us are overwhelmed by the sense that no one ever has—or ever could—hear us as well as this newly beloved. To both partners' frustration, however, the pillow-talk days go fleetingly by. Without a commitment to both emotional integrity and deep listening, the thrill of *truly* hearing our partner inevitably gets lost as our simpatico feelings for each other become diluted by less fun, more complex feelings.

Eventually, as lovemates make their inexorable passage into the power-struggle stage of relationship (sometimes remaining stranded there for years), they lose the ability to listen to each other at all. Each partner "hears" not what was said but what was feared or expected. A woman who spent her childhood being blamed for every last little thing, for example, hears accusation in a partner's concern over a child's school performance. A man who wishes desperately that he could spend more time with the kids hears blame in his wife's compassionate comment about his schedule. As a result of such miscommunications, partners vacillate between the wildest emotional extremes and tightest shutdown of feelings in their adult lives.

Is the problem inevitable? As we've said, all relationships pass into the power struggle, but this transit need not be as brutal as it usually is. The key is preserving trust. That's why the Law of Deep Listening addresses everything to do with trust—building it, breaking it, and eventually, with or without facilitation, rebuilding it.

Let's take a closer look at that sequence. In the intoxication stage of relationship, this special kind of listening is how we first learn to trust each other. Later, during the power struggle, buttons and blind spots start to crowd out real relating. Not knowing how to take responsibility for our emotions, we inevitably start manipulating, nagging, and otherwise acting out our unlovable feelings. As listeners, our first defense to those behaviors in a partner is to unwittingly tune him or her out; trust then falls by the wayside. But lovers can learn to listen again, deeply listen, and by honoring each other's heartfelt communications, they can rebuild trust.

Deep listening puts some demands on the speaker as well: all communication of feelings need be in the form of I-statements expressed in a reasonable tone of voice and supplemented with nonthreatening body language. Raging decibels and bulging neck veins don't make for responsible expression; language, tone of voice, and posture work together to encourage safe, respectful emotional dialogue. Here's the bottom line: *As a rule, if you're on the receiving end and are frightened by any communication from your mate, deep listening isn't appropriate.* What's called for instead is a time-out, a primary tool used in anger management (a subject to be discussed in Chapter 6, "Peacemaking").

If deep listening doesn't happen even when the communicator speaks gently and sticks to I-statements, there may be an underlying problem. An inability to tolerate responsibly expressed anger may be a symptom of unhealed childhood trauma—a parent who had episodes of explosive rage, for example. The wounded partner needs to take responsibility for that traumatic button and work with a therapist to address the issue.

Self-Love Loves Deep Listening

One major benefit of deep listening is its tendency to elevate our self-love. In that regard it works wonders. Deep listening is the same process by which parents create high self-love in their children and therapists help their clients recover from deficient self-love (and a variety of other emotional ills). When parents are able to validate and encourage the expression of their children's full rainbow of feelings, they help to create the initial sense of self-worth. These little ones then grow up with the healthy conviction that they deserve all forms of safety and respect, and without the excessive need for external approval. They're convinced from the outset of the value of their own feelings, thoughts, and intuition—indeed, of their very value as human beings.

Deep listening is also how parents minimize the traumatic impact on their children of life's scrapes, falls, and tragedies—and the technique works well for couples, too. Its success lies in the fact that when, as children, we're encouraged by emotionally integrated parents to tell the story of our pain, we can to a large degree let it go. The words "emotionally integrated" are key here, because parents—like love partners—are capable of listening to the emotions of others only to the extent that they've already accepted their own. We can assume, then, that if our parents couldn't listen to us, their parents couldn't listen to them.

Children who grow up with unlistening parents mature into adults who have an intense need to be heard. While when it comes to exploring trauma, a trusted psychotherapist is our best ear, partners can still listen far more fully to each other's emotional truth than most of us currently do. Using our skills of deep listening in combination with the skills and commitments outlined in the Law of Emotional Integrity, we can create an emotionally safe atmosphere that allows us to deal with blind spots and buttons, resolve new conflict, rebuild trust, and shore up sagging self-love.

Giving the Greatest Gift of Love

Whereas one member of a couple might be more naturally gifted as a listener than the other, both can learn to listen emotionally and with competence. As with all the skills in this book, the willingness to try is paramount. And that willingness can be triggered in a partner by our own modeling. Perhaps, the greatest inspiration for learning to really listen is having been on the receiving end—having ourselves been heard in this loving fashion.

Deep listening is a gift of attention, of staying present—emotionally, mentally, and when possible with our eyes—as our mate relates information that he or she considers important. It's this perception of importance that gives any message its emotional weight. And it's our self-discipline as listeners—restraining ourselves from interrupting, judging, advising, or intervening in any way—that makes the speaker feel not only emotionally "held" but also honored. When the speaker uses I-statements as much as possible and avoids acting out, all the listener has to do is sit tight.

Deep listening doesn't ask you to interview or mirror your mate or to listen either actively or reflectively, as some other listening techniques do. Both partners just have to agree to be attentive while the other is talking. Of course, timing is always a consideration. If the moment isn't good, we need to say so, suggesting an alternate time when we'd be able to lend a loving ear (or preferably two).

Some of us, however, will find that even after practicing, we just can't deeply listen to our mate; we can't help but interrupt, perhaps, or we have trouble sitting still, being present, making eye contact, or otherwise staying focused. Since a problem of that nature is always an issue of buttons or blind spots, we can roll this issue over to the tenth Natural Law of Love and sign up for some Help.

Deep listening can happen anywhere: in the tent you pitched for the kids in the yard, in the car during your commute to work, or on a back-country trail; it can even happen over the phone in a pinch, if circumstances don't allow for face-to-face conversation. If we use this skill judiciously, we find that deep listening, like I-statements, can become part of the natural music of our couple's conversation. Though we don't interact via deep listening all the time, our use of this practice will have a cumulative effect on our relationship. Over time, it will instill in any couple a profound mutual respect.

The Session: In Search of a Loving Ear

The best way two people can get trained in the art of deep listening—not to mention handling common communication breakdowns—is through learning (and then incorporating into the relationship) an exercise called "the Session." This amazingly simple tool was born of great personal necessity for us. We were on the beaches of southern Thailand, one scant year into our marriage and six months into a year-long trip around world. Though we were often in each other's exclusive company twenty-four hours a day, we found ourselves growing apart—one of us becoming slightly agitated, the other somewhat sullen, and both losing interest in sharing what was really going on.

How could this be, we wondered? Here we were, two trained listeners and supposed experts in providing emotional support, yet we were shutting down on each other on the biggest adventure of our lives. At first we thought that we needed couple counseling, but this was logistically impossible. Then it occurred to us to counsel each other, but this was therapeutically impossible. To our amazement, we found an alternative way to build a bridge back to each other.

What we felt we needed was sacred space—in other words, an opportunity to talk and be heard without commentary, feedback, or facilitation. The result was the Session, and it revived—indeed, transformed—the quality of our relating (not to mention saving our trip!). It doesn't involve therapy, counseling, or any mirroring or similar exercise requiring interpersonal finesse. Rather, the Session asks for two loving ears, an open heart, and hundred-percent undivided attention for as little as ten minutes per person. Since we discovered this miraculous exercise, we've not only taught it to countless couples, but fifteen years later we still do it ourselves two to three times a week. Here's how the Session works:

> **The two partners arrange a block of time for their Session, allowing a minimum of twenty minutes so that both partners get at least ten minutes of listening time. They can go longer if they like—in fact, twenty minutes per person is ideal—as long as both get equal time, *no exceptions*. Timekeeping is the Listener's responsibility.**

The Session takes place in a private, quiet area. Eliminate all disruptions and distractions: turn off telephone ringers, pagers, televisions, radios, stereos, and turn down the answering machine; ignore the doorbell; and if children are in the picture, make sure they're safely looked after. This is intimate time and must be treated as precious. Don't drink alcohol prior to a Session, and no snacking, drinking, or smoking during a Session. The point is for partners to be as present as possible for each other.

The first Speaker talks about whatever he or she wishes, including the events of the day, feelings from the past, or issues involving the relationship. The only exception is any topic about which the Speaker is angry at the Listener. This topic should be saved for the Path to Peace, detailed in Chapter 6, "Peacemaking." This is a crucial judgment call. Because the Session is a precious tool that can dramatically enhance trust and intimacy, it's worth using correctly.

Partners should avoid blame and you-statements (e.g., "You don't like my cooking"). Instead, they should use I-statements with specific feelings (e.g., "I feel sad that you didn't like the lasagna"). Positive feelings should be included too (e.g., "I loved how you surprised me at work today" or "I was so proud of how you managed your anger in the car"). If the Speaker runs out of things to say before his or her allotted time is up, both partners sit in silence making eye contact.

The Listener's job is simply to listen with eyes, heart, and full attention, imagining that by listening to the beloved, he or she is giving a beautiful gift. The Listener is not to respond or talk under any circumstances, except to ask the Speaker to repeat something that was inaudible.

When the Speaker's time is over, both partners switch roles. The second Speaker can't use this turn to respond to the first person's words, however. That response should be saved until the next Session.

> Once both partners have had a turn, the Session is over. To provide a sense of completion, they may choose to thank each other and hug.

At first, some partners find speaking—and being listened to—for ten or fifteen minutes without interruption a little awkward. In addition, some initially find that the format feels a little artificial or contrived. It's a good idea, then, to commit to at least three Sessions per week for one month. This is usually enough to get the kinks out of the system and allay any discomfort. As people get used to the Session, they often realize that in *normal* conversation they're so preoccupied with what they themselves are going to say next that they barely hear their partner. By tying the Listener's tongue, the Session deals with that preoccupation. Likewise, the Session keeps people from jumping in with solutions.

Sessions have the impressive ability to lighten the load for each partner; they also help us feel closer than ever. When our lover just listens, it's possible to get in touch with how we really feel. And that genuine emotion might just surprise us. In the guaranteed silence, jumbles of feelings (some of which we didn't even know we felt) often get sorted through; mini-insights, great epiphanies, even brainstorm solutions to thorny problems frequently make themselves known. In addition, the Session dissipates day-to-day free-floating stress. Finally, Sessions serve to remind us that, as lovemates, we're honored to gingerly and reverently hold the contents of each other's heart.

Even just a few experiences with the Session can be powerful. Each time we're the Speaker, we increase our levels of emotional awareness, emotional fluency, and emotional honesty—each of which augments self-love. With practice, we start to listen deeply to each other as a matter of course, both in and out of Session.

Once we've reached that level of greater comfort with the basic Session, we can choose to schedule "Special Sessions" for matters of particular concern or issues on which we have strongly differing opinions (as long as we don't feel at risk of acting out over those issues). Special Sessions might be focused on problems at work or with the kids, for example, or on future plans—even life dreams. Special Sessions are exceptional in that the Listener has permission to respond to what the Speaker said when it's his or her turn to talk. They're exceptional in their level of accomplishment as well: when we provide each other with this kind of open space, perplexing problems often find easy resolution.

Deep Listening Over Traditional Communication

The traditional couple was too often the lonely couple. In days gone by, deep listening, like all interpersonal and couple skills, was a foreign notion to most spouses. And since higher-order needs were equally exotic, the emotional alienation created by this listening vacuum wasn't considered abnormal. Indeed, other than certain tender wives and still fewer tender husbands, traditional couples had little conception that a specific way to pay heed to each other existed. The possibility of deep listening's gifts—maintaining and rebuilding trust, making and keeping the peace, and enhancing self-worth—was even farther from their minds.

Typically, neither traditional spouse felt listened to, much less empathized with. Men were often doubled over in toxic shame about their personal problems and feelings. They ended up telling their woes to the local barber or bartender, if anyone. Women fared somewhat better in the expression of emotions. Since the culture didn't shame them so intensely for their feelings, they were freer to share them. Often they listened to each other, seeking support from their family-of-origin, hairdresser, or coffee klatch. With this separation along gender lines, the traditional arrangement deprived both sexes of a brilliant best friend—that is, the beloved other; and in many quarters it still does.

Naturally, these unfair gender patterns imprinted the next generation. As a result, father-son relationships were impoverished.

Many boys couldn't tell their fathers how they felt because their fathers didn't know how to listen. And if they'd tried a few times and failed, they sure weren't going to risk another disappointment! Unwittingly, these fathers set their sons up, not only to repeat their own isolation but also to serve in their stead: these youngsters were recruited by their mothers, who yearned for a male ear, to fill the role of confidant. Though unintentional, this command-performance closeness was burdensome and unhealthy for boys, who shouldn't have been in the mix when it came to maternal emotional needs. What loving son could refuse his mother— at least at first? But because many wanted to refuse, this all-too-common scenario caused boys to grow up with a distaste for feelings or even a simmering resentment of women in general.

Daughters of the traditional couple didn't do much better. Like their brothers, they didn't really expect their fathers to listen to them. This low expectation seriously undermined their confidence in the importance of their own feelings and opinions and sent them subtle but destructive messages about "normal" relationships with men. Girls grew up to accept strong, silent types and jokers (who'd distract instead of listen). Again like their brothers, they were often conscripted into service as their mother's—and sometimes their father's—chosen listener. Some weren't even allowed to make deep connections among their peers.

As unaware of the principle of emotional integrity as they were of the Law of Deep Listening, traditional couples frequently acted their feelings out rather than expressing them verbally. As we mentioned in the previous chapter, this made the expression of feelings traumatic to their children. Often individual partners came from families where anger wore the face of rage, fear the face of neurosis, or sadness the face of depression. Given that background, even spouses who expressed the less-pleasant feelings to each other in a nonadversarial fashion triggered fear. Staying shut down, tuned out, or perpetually busy—in short, doing everything in their power to avoid listening to each other—was thus a simple matter of self-preservation.

When couple psychology finally made its debut in the mid-sixties, the importance of an emotion-focused listening emerged. "He [or she] doesn't care about my feelings; she [or he] never listens to me" became the anthem for troubled relationships. Indeed, it seemed that—regardless of whether there was violence, alcoholism, or philandering—the demise of every marriage was attributed to a breakdown in emotional communication.

Even without complications such as violence or alcoholism, couples struggling with higher-level dialogue still had a hard time of it. Diagnosis was definitely not cure; to many mates' great disappointment, knowing that they needed to open up their mouths and their ears didn't rescue their marriage. Some were still unwilling or unable to be aware of, talk about, or be honest regarding their feelings. Others still just couldn't listen. The pileups of the infamous power-struggle stage (many caused by unhealed childhood wounds, as we've seen) tended to preclude successful communication.

Fortunately, the New Couple need never be the lonely couple. That's due in large part to the benefits of deep listening. Long the basic counseling skill, deep listening is primed to become the couple skill as well, for clearly the power of this fourth Natural Law of Love to transform any relationship—not least of which are our love unions—is phenomenal. When we commit to learning to listen to each other from the heart, we can rest assured that, no matter what happens outside, *we will be heard at home.* Our couple might then become the first place where we've ever experienced truly loving attention and respect, advancing both our self-love and emotional intimacy light years ahead. What could be a greater gift of love?

As couple skills go, deep listening is relatively straightforward. For certain of us, however, its acquisition may require more patience and discipline than for others. Some of us might even need additional instruction—or healing—before we can really get it down. Soon, though, we'll see the benefits of learning to allow for the more general expression of feelings in our relationship.

Started early and continued through the life of the relationship, deep listening reduces the chances that the din of the power struggle—amplified by all its blind spots, buttons, and issues—will deafen us both. When, as a New Couple, we both commit to ratchet our hearing up one notch, we're practicing prevention whether we realize it or not. Because of our sensitive hearing, innumerable gusts and flurries of stress will be imperceptibly, yet continuously, blown off course and away. We'll never even know the storms that might have occurred. In addition, deep listening protects us when small squalls do blow our way, ensuring that little experiences of not being heard don't grow into perceived massive betrayals.

As an easy couple tool, the Session stands in a league of one. A great training ground for learning the skill of deep listening, it also functions as a daily stress reducer par excellence. Countless couples have found the Session to be eminently worth the tiny expenditure of their time—twenty to thirty minutes. And the effort required for love's sake—biting our tongues, keeping our opinions to ourselves, and letting our lover source his or her own solutions (and feelings)—pays amazing dividends. In fact, deep listening is unbelievably economical: we can reduce stress, solve problems, avoid fights, and raise our self-love—all while vastly enhancing our overall ability to be emotionally intimate. We might even save money on therapy!

If we let the fourth Natural Law of Love help us stay tuned to the truth of our beloved's mind and heart, we'll soon see how the habit of lending an ear unreservedly, and really making the beloved's emotions feel at home with us, can seal our friendship for life.

THE KEY TO DEEP LISTENING

Learning the skill of listening to your partner straight from the heart—that is, listening for the words and the feelings underneath with compassion—is the key to the fourth Natural Law of Love. This means holding ...

- Sessions on a regular basis

- Special Sessions as needed

If you think that the concept of Equality in love partnerships is as warmed-over as a peace sign, you're right. As *concepts*, both have been kicked around at least since the sixties, when a number of bras and flags went up in flames.

Today, diversity is the watchword in Western society, and discrimination of any kind is still highly politically incorrect. As *realities*, however, neither equality nor peace between lovers is yet fully realized.

It's true that couples who openly embrace the kind of traditional marriage where gender dictates both the balance of power and the playing of roles are now the exception. It's also true that most couples strongly defend the fact of equality in their own partnership. Nonetheless, inequality *still persists* in almost every realm of connubial life. And since we need to be equals before we can fly a peace flag over our household, the Law of Equality is the fifth Natural Law of Love, preceding the Law of Peacemaking.

There are a host of standard measures by which the power within a relationship is determined—measures such as age, gender, race, religion, ethnicity, financial status, income-generating potential, socioeconomic background, gifts, talents, physical health and abilities, and intellectual prowess. Though we've come a long way in our thinking about how these measures affect the roles and responsibilities of coupledom, who among us can say that we've reached an honest balance when it comes to the daunting list of specifics, including moneymaking, household management and repairs, errands, car maintenance, manual labor and physical security, lovemaking, parenting, childcare and education, family-of-origin relations, and caring for aging parents? Clearly, we have a long way to go.

Though the label may suggest it, the Law of Equality isn't specifically intended to raise the status of women to that of men in heterosexual relationships. It goes way beyond that. This law concerns itself with a standard of fairness in all love unions for both sexes. It asks us to take responsibility for how the power is distributed in our couple—in other words, who's got the clout—and to make sure we both consider the distribution fair. If we discover a glimmer of sexism along the way, it's up to us to take care of it.

Expectations are Premeditated Resentments
—12-Step Axiom

Equality—which is integral to respect and love of self and other—also requires that we approach all conjugal roles and responsibilities without assumption or expectation. In other words, nothing is presumed; both partners have an equal voice, and *everything*—from finances to cooking to who picks up the children at school—is negotiable. The only exception is core agreements, which are nonnegotiable. (These will be discussed in Chapter 6, "Peacemaking," along with negotiation itself.)

In practice, the Law of Equality invites us to do the following:

Honestly examine the major facets of shared life and acknowledge those in which the power is out of balance. A couple might realize, for example, that a discrepancy in age has thrown off their balance of power.

Explore how this "advantage" might translate to unfairness for one or both partners. To continue our example, the younger partner might realize that he or she automatically defers to the decisions of the older.

Get in touch with, and share, any feelings associated with this dynamic, negative and positive. In our example, the younger partner might feel relief at not having a lot of responsibility, resentment at not being trusted with responsibility, and fear that the disempowerment is justified because of incompetence. The older partner, who enjoys a certain amount of freedom in not having to negotiate, might also feel resentful of the burden and guilty for being domineering.

Offer a good-faith promise (backed by specifics) to restore harmony and/or negotiate toward fairness. Our couple above, having mutually agreed that things were unfair, might commit to start paying attention to how decisions evolve between them and to negotiate as needed. They might also make a date in a week's time to see how they're doing.

This process isn't appropriate in every situation of inequality, of course. We can work out many issues without turning them into questions of equality—the trading off of shopping for unloading and putting the groceries away, for example. Other issues are too complex to be handled by the Law of Equality alone. For example, when only one of us perceives an imbalance and we're not able to come to agreement, we need to apply the conflict-resolution skills presented in the next chapter.

As you can see, New Couples manage power through conversation—actually, a series of ongoing conversations. The topics of the equality discussion revolve around all the power issues mentioned earlier—differences in age, gender, moneymaking ability, intelligence, and so on—and any unfairness they cause in the relationship. Talks about all kinds of responsibility, but especially the touchy main issues (such as the day-to-day earning and management of money, the care and rearing of children, and good old house-work), are essential to the Natural Law of Equality.

Some areas of responsibility are typically shared, while others are taken on by one or the other of us as a specialty. And that's fine: equality doesn't require matching responsibilities; it asks only that nothing be assumed and everything be open to negotiation. Some power imbalances need to be rectified; others—those that don't create any hard feelings—need simply to be acknowledged. What's key is how both partners *honestly feel* about any issue of power.

It's important to remember that, like the other nine Natural Laws of Love, equality is an ideal. It doesn't require a ten-out-of-ten performance, just a heartfelt commitment on the part of both partners.

Equality's Greatest Challenge

THE TRANCE OF TRADITION

Unfortunately, filling this prescription for fairness can be tricky. We all come to relationships with various superiority and inferiority complexes, feeling sure of ourselves in some ways and unsure in others. We might know, for example, that we're better at sports, worth more on the job market, or less silver-tongued than our beloved. Still, as we've said, our hearts are generally in the right place, and the unfairness that crops up between us typically isn't deliberate. *Rather, inequality generally results from unspoken tolerance of unnegotiated assignments of responsibility based on traditional* (read: gender) *roles.* In fact, the strong hold that the notorious trance of tradition has on the Law of Equality is equaled only by its hold on the Law of Priority, specifically on the challenging process of individuation that Priority involves.

And yet the responsibility for inequality falls squarely on our own shoulders: when we function discontentedly in a capacity that we accepted without question, doing nothing to correct the situation, we're imposing inequality on *ourselves*. As has been so wisely remarked, "No one can take our power away; we've got to give it away." Similarly, when we're in an ostensibly equal couple, no one can impose a role or duty upon us if we're not willing to accept it.

More often than not, though, home duties such as housecleaning or lawnmowing are divvied up unconsciously, without much thought and certainly without negotiation. Locked in the trance of tradition, partners simply step into certain roles. Part cultural, part psychological, traditional roles begin to take hold of us when, as children, we're imprinted with traditional mores. We watch our parents function according to overt and unspoken rules, biases, and notions of status passed down through family, religion, and ethnic group. Often we're also directly or indirectly encouraged to keep these conventions up ourselves.

Like DNA, such internalized ideas contain very specific information—details about how we, as men, women, husbands, and wives, should behave in our relationships. These stereotypes generally lie dormant until the stress of the power struggle hits or we have children (two events that sometimes coincide or collide). At those high-pressure times of life, we start unconsciously seeking what's safe and known: before we realize it, we're betraying unnegotiated expectations about equal responsibility and power and are defaulting back into the spousal roles of those who raised us.

When that happens, we know we've got problems with equality blind spots. Blinding as the glaring sun, these rob us of the awareness of what's fair; they press buttons and set our relationship up for trouble. Like emotional blind spots, they require the honest communication of our feelings.

Striving for Equality in Parenting and Finances

Unquestionably, cultural programming and early wounding pile a lot on our plates. And couples who decide to marry and have kids find that their challenges are quadrupled. The problem isn't just the centripetal force of tradition; it's also socioeconomics and the family-hostile structure of the workaday world.

Unless we're self-employed or independently wealthy, we may feel that the odds are stacked against us, no matter how deeply we care about transcending gender inequalities—not to mention creating a new, fair kind of family where both parents contribute equally to the financial picture and the raising of children. Facing the three modern-family monsters of finances, childrearing, and household management (not to mention a no-pun-intended laundry list of other related duties), those of us committed to each other without heeding equality and sharing might, to our horror, suddenly find ourselves severely equality-challenged,

Pragmatically, it's easier by far to collapse into traditional caregiver/breadwinner roles—and emotionally, to let the chips fall where they may.

Many couples consciously decide, once their first child is on its way, to go with the traditional formula, figuring that they can tweak it here and there to allow the father more time at home and the mother more time away. Although the arrangement often works well for men, women are typically torn between wanting the "housewife" role and wanting to begin a career or resume their professional life.

This pull isn't uncommon. On the one hand, the vulnerability of nesting causes us to cling tenaciously to custom—a tendency that's especially strong in people suffering (knowingly or unknowingly) from childhood emotional neglect or abandonment trauma. On the other hand, as parenthood deepens and strengthens the trance of tradition—with all its latent expectations about roles and responsibilities—we find some of our contemporary personal values squarely in opposition to those of tradition.

Even when both partners earn enough individually so that

either one could choose to stay home with the children—meaning that the couple could switch caregiver/breadwinner roles after the nursing period if they wanted to—men rarely choose the home role. The question isn't whether having the mother at home and the father at work is good for the children, for certainly it's fine; rather, it's whether the decision for him to stay duly employed and for her to stay at home has been negotiated. Is the choice based on true preferences or on the trance of tradition (as embodied in equality blind spots)?

In planning for families, few of us sit down to have that "big talk" together. It's the exceptional couple who examine how the traditional arrangement might affect them—how it might, for example, cut off their chance to experience a novel family life in which the father is at least as involved with the children as the mother is. While men don't often take the opportunity to delve into total-involvement parenting (and rarely even see it as an option), men who've really considered being a New Dad report feelings from curiosity and excitement to foreboding. Almost invariably, however, they also experience some level of discomfort with the unmacho implications of not being out in the world like most guys; many are downright afraid of being judged by colleagues, friends, and family, and of the toxic shame the judgment might evoke. That would perhaps change, of course, if employers automatically granted fathers the two or three months of maternity leave that women typically get.

When a couple opts for what's familiar without finding out what they truly desire, without experimenting and negotiating, one or both partners generally end up feeling victimized and resentful. If the habit of ceding to unarticulated pressures regarding outmoded, unnegotiated roles continues unchallenged over the years, it has the potential to damage a couple's chemistry—sometimes irreparably.

As this discussion shows, equality is all about the *politics* and *power* of relationship. In the context of love, however, neither term need be a dirty word. When we acknowledge power issues up front, openly discussing "who's got what," we significantly diminish the likelihood that our wonderful, God-given strengths and advantages will devolve into tools of manipulation. We're able to transform what might have become dirty politics into the politics of peace and love. Furthermore, a genuine effort to embrace the Law of Equality can have a profound impact on preserving our all-important chemistry, elevating our self-love, and building our trust.

Making Equality a Reality

The original institution of marriage wasn't created for equals—and rarely was it fair.

How could spouses possibly see to the equitable distribution of power in their relationship when the power had already been parceled out—by society and religion? It was often *might* that made *right*: the partner who could outmuscle, outearn, outsmart, outspeak, or otherwise outmaneuver the other pulled the strings.

These paradigms notwithstanding, our own parents and grandparents would probably have said that they considered themselves equals—just different in terms of the roles they played. That's because they themselves bought into society's delegation of power. Grievances related to imbalances in age, money, employment status, and family background weren't routinely aired, let alone redressed; they were left to fester. Bottom line? Even though most traditional spouses didn't have the luxury of questioning marital inequalities—and wouldn't have admitted to them anyway—they must have known, in their heart of hearts, that none of the above was particularly fair.

For example, many women felt disempowered by their dearth of marketable skills, wondering how they'd put bread on the table if their husbands left for greener pastures. Many men, for their part, were so accustomed to subduing their feelings and running the office that they extended that control impulse to home duties and finances. Both genders were unsatisfied, but because traditional spouses were strangers to emotional honesty, deep listening, and the principles of the Law of Equality, they had no idea how to make things fair.

Because partners today have tools that previous generations lacked, the New Couple has the courage to be fair—to themselves and each other. And when it comes to putting together the nuts and bolts of their partnership, they start from scratch. They see the folly and injustice of prefab role assignments and notions of status or superiority. Still, they grapple with the blind spots that the Law of Equality warns about—blind spots regarding conjugal roles and responsibilities and differing abilities and advantages. They're not looking for a perfect score or trying to measure up to anyone else's standards; instead, they're looking for what's fair from their own individual vantage points.

The straight path to equality is and always will be through open-hearted conversation, brokered using the skills of emotional literacy, honesty, and management, along with deep listening. While we can talk about some issues early in the relationship—age and earning power, for example—others just come up when they do. The goal is to talk about them as early as possible and to be as honest as possible. It's best not to wait until the power struggle sets in, because by that time our talents and advantages might have soured into liabilities, and unnegotiated responsibilities and expectations might already have gotten both partners' backs up.

Let's look at how two couples dealt with the issue of equality in Special Sessions. These Sessions, excerpted here for brevity, share the common themes of insecurities about major differences and expectations of self or other based on family and cultural conditioning. (Remember that in Special Sessions, unlike regular Sessions, the Listener can respond to what the Speaker said when it's his or her turn to talk.)

Financial Status and Closet Sexism

Corey had just been promoted to the position of vice president of the aggressive retail chain for which he'd worked for five years. Wei Ling, his wife, was a historian who managed a flower shop part-time; financially, this latter was almost purely a labor of love. To her husband's dismay, she seemed dedicated to becoming an eternal student as well. Still, in many ways this couple personified the progressive marriage. For example, they had no problem splitting chores right down the middle.

Though their house was deeded to Wei Ling, part of her settlement from a previous marriage, it was Corey who handled the mortgage payments and related expenses. Eating out, holidays, and all extras also seemed to come down to him, though for some reason they'd both remained mute on the subject for the first seven years of their marriage. It wasn't until Wei Ling announced her intention to take out a loan for a second master's degree that Corey put his cards on the table. He scheduled a Special Session on the topic of their financial future—and past.

Corey began: "You know I really appreciate this great old house you've provided us, Wei Ling, and I want to support you in your interests. But we've never really gotten clear about our roles in terms of finances. I don't want to stress you out, but I don't want to start holding the money issue against you, either. It's true that I should have mentioned it before, but I guess I was waiting for you to—which isn't fair. It's not that I don't like my job, but now you're talking about another degree, more debt, and no end in sight—and there seems to be an assumption that I'm going to continue to foot all the bills. What if I wanted to leave my job? I'd be trapped. I wonder if you ever plan to participate in our major expenses. A part of me—I guess it's old-fashioned—thinks that ultimately the financial buck stops with me, and I feel guilty and ungenerous in even bringing it up."

Wei Ling lowered her eyes: "You're right. I feel nervous and guilty too, talking about this. I try to push the question of our finances out of my mind when it comes up, or I make myself feel better by the thought that the house is mine. And I keep hoping you won't notice or mind that I'm not pulling my weight financially. I know I'm not being realistic—or fair to you. I guess it's partly my upbringing. Even though I call myself a feminist and believe that women should have not only equal rights but equal responsibilities, there's a part of me that just plain resents men. I'm not proud of how I feel, but it's like, Well, they control the economy, so they should bear the brunt of the bills. Pretty hypocritical, huh? I feel embarrassed that I don't make as much money as you do. I'm afraid that even if I tried, I couldn't come near your income. Staying a student is safe; that way I never have to find out what I'm capable of."

Corey's face was open and full of love when he responded: "That's all I wanted to hear. I don't want you to get a job you hate or to grovel. We'll work the details out. Still, I really needed for us to clear the air. You're truly amazing. Who'd have thought we'd both have such sneaky inner sexists, or that they'd be running our show?"

Assumptions about Gender-Based Knowledge

Hazel and Eli couldn't contain the joy they felt at the birth of their twin boys. A computer programmer, she'd been lucky to get an open-ended leave of absence from work. Meantime, Eli, a plumbing contractor, had added hours and now was working time and a half. Caring for two babies single-handedly while Eli was at work ten hours a day proved too heavy a workload for Hazel—and she let her husband know it. Even so, when it was Eli's turn to help out with the kids, he'd hold Ogden the "wrong" way or forget to put talcum powder on Chester's bottom. Hazel just didn't seem able to cut him any slack; she was always on his case. Confused and frustrated, Eli requested a Special Session limited to the subject of co-parenting.

Eli jumped right in: "Hazel, hon, I know you feel overwhelmed by the boys. Your long days are rough. In fact, I don't know how you keep your patience with the babies, even with your mother and sister helping out. Honestly, I wouldn't want to change places with you if I could. Still, we're supposed to be partners in this. When I'm home at night, I'm as committed and available as any dad could be. I love those little guys, and I want to father them! But sometimes you act as though I can't do anything right. I've read all the books too, but you give me the impression I'm undoing everything you learned in your New Mother classes. I don't necessarily agree with you every time, either. I bite my tongue because I don't want bad vibes around the babies. That I'm positive is bad for them. Anyway, thanks for hearing me out."

Hazel looked perplexed. "Am I really that bad?" she asked. "I know that I don't seem able to control my anxiety about doing everything perfectly for the boys. I watch myself hassling you and I know it's unfair. I'm driving myself bonkers too! I seem to be turning into a control-freak mom. My mother sort of drummed it into my head that men don't have the maternal instinct. My father wasn't allowed to set foot in the nursery—but of course, unlike you, he didn't want to. I thought that was bizarre. I know that studies have proven some children are actually better off with their father functioning as primary parent. The conditioning is definitely in me, though—it's like I have a superiority complex when it comes to parenting. I owe it to all three of my men to get a handle on it."

When we commit to equality within the couple—and face the potentially volatile subjects of power and politics head on—we're actually pioneering a new way: the way to fairness and true equality between partners.

We're acknowledging that the traditional paradigm, with its anachronistic expectations and assumptions about conjugal roles and responsibilities, has been burned into the unconscious of lovers for too long (and is too potent) to be fully shed in a single generation. We're also demonstrating a wise awareness that, unless openly and lovingly discussed, the weighting of any kind of power to one side of our couple will ignite insecurities and resentments with long-term ill-effects.

When inequality blind spots do turn up, as they inevitably will in even the most vigilant couples, a generous helping of forgiveness – for ourselves and our partner — is the first step. We make huge headway, however, just by being sensitive to how imbalances and expectations affect us and our beloved. Our skills of emotional literacy, honesty, and management will serve us well as we sit down together for those little chats and big talks, as will our ability to listen deeply. However, since equality and fairness tend to create complexity, a new kind of conversational structure is often required. The negotiation skills and couple agreements presented in the next chapter are invaluable in building that new structure.

It takes guts to truly embrace a standard of fairness, but when we make equality a central plank in our platform, our New Couple is well on its way to success.

THE KEY TO EQUALITY

Insisting on fairness and respect for yourself and your partner is the key to the fifth Natural Law of Love.

This means. . . .

- 🖤 Honestly examining and sharing your feelings about differences, expectations and assumptions, and unnegotiated roles and responsibilities, along with any unfairness that results from these.

- 🖤 Committing to rectify unfairness to both partners' satisfaction.

PEACEMAKING

If the technology of war seems out of control in the world, at least the technology of peace is well within reach—that is, within the privacy and sanctity of coupledom.

This sixth Natural Law of Love—the Law of Peacemaking—picks up where emotional integrity, deep listening, and equality leave off. Peacemaking offers us the power tools we need to transform our relationship into an emotional safe zone. It handles our buttons and blind spots by asking us to create couple agreements and learn a set of skills designed to help us manage anger and resolve conflict.

As with all New Couple skills, we gain competence at making and keeping the peace gradually. We practice, falteringly at first, and then one fine day our hard work pays off: we notice that peacemaking has imperceptibly become integral to the fabric of our relationship—the natural way we react to each other in testy moments. With the Law of Peacemaking, it's not whether we get in trouble that matters, for it's assumed we will. What's important is how we get out of trouble.

Those who've enjoyed the bonding experience of a well-resolved fight might already be able to imagine the potency of the peacemaking process. Peacemaking has the ability not only to transform relational fissures into some of our greatest strengths as a couple, but also to fortify our relationship overall. And the effort required is quite minimal—a matter of seconds to manage anger, and about ten minutes to get over most tiffs—considering that this could well be the most important human technology we ever master.

The first component of this law, *core agreements*, represents our own personal conditions for a relationship—that is, our individual bottom line. Some core agreements are recommended by the Law of Peacemaking, and some will be written by each individual. The second component, *anger management*, requires a skill and several additional agreements. These agreements, however, are part of a technique, and they're prewritten; the skill asks only that, when the time is right, we utter—rather emphatically—two tiny but potent words. The final part of peacemaking, *conflict resolution*, employs another technique, this one deceptively simple, which we can either verbalize or write to our mates. Sometimes it's necessary that we formulate additional negotiable agreements in order to arrive at what's truly fair for both of us; at other times it's necessary for us to make amends.

If it sounds like making and keeping the peace in a couple requires scads of agreements, that's true. Still, the bulk of the agreements are negotiable even after they're in place, and the number any couple needs is up to the two of them. The multitude of agreements needed is evidence of one of the primary lessons this chapter hopes to teach: to be successful, equal partnership has to be an ongoing negotiation. And what we'll never know until we try is that some of the mutual wins we arrive at via negotiation may prove to be absolutely brilliant, making us better friends than ever.

Despite the reasonableness of such an approach, some of us may not be comfortable with the idea of a predesigned method to promote and maintain peace in an intimate relationship. As was explained in Chapter 3—Emotional Intrgrity, a particularly traumatic childhood can strongly predispose some of us to "white-knuckle it." Riddled with buttons and blind spots, we end up conflict- and anger-avoidant, or (opting for an opposite approach) perhaps quietly or explosively "rageaholic," or even both at different times. Frequently, these opposite types marry. The tendency toward either type is especially strong in those who (whether they remember it or not) were subjected as kids to shaming or guilt for having or expressing feelings, or were subjected to psychological, verbal, or physical acting out of anger.

Those of us who avoid anger and conflict are often afraid that if we get near either one, we'll get hurt or turn into abusers ourselves. Those of us who can't control our rage often secretly fear that we'll fail if we try. Whichever type we are, we deserve compassion and patience, for clearly we've already been through enough. Eventually, though, we would all do well to face such fears—an endeavor that could transform our lives. But the choice is ours: it's up to each of us as individuals to opt for either the way of making and keeping peace, or life in a relationship without the technology of peace.

Creating Core Agreements

DRAWING LINES IN THE SAND

While most of us have relegated *unconditional love* to the domain of angels and bodhisattvas and are reconciled to experiencing only a shimmering moment of such love from time to time, we have yet to give up on the idea of *unconditional relationship*. We claim that it's uptight and legalistic to set conditions in our relationship; we see such conditions as signs of bad faith or lack of trust in our mate. We worry that setting conditions within the relationship puts unfair demands on our partner.

In fact, a successful relationship without real conditions is to us mortal couples as elusive as a perpetual state of unconditional love. Why so? Because, as the street wisdom goes, *where there are no rules, we tend to make up our own—individually*. Though the notion of rules is inappropriately harsh for love unions, it must be said that when no conditions are articulated within a couple, assumptions abound. And it follows that when no conversations take place to deal with equality issues, for example, each partner may assume that the other will take responsibility. For one of us the resulting assumption might read, When the doorbell rings, the person closest to the door answer it, while the other partner's assumption might read, The man always answers the door. The confusion and conflict that result from unspoken assumptions bring out the worst in of all of us—bully, victim, nag, Peter Pan, martyr, guilt-tripper, master manipulator.

If, on the other hand, we do set conditions in our relationship—and these are honored as agreements—our self-esteem flourishes. This in turn brings out the best in both of us. Indeed, though it may seem paradoxical, a few seriously self-loving conditions are the best way for us to open the floodgates to blissfully unconditional mutual regard.

Specifically, the Law of Peacemaking proposes that, *as individuals*, each of us identify those conditions that we know we can't live without in our union. These are called the *core conditions* for the relationship. Ideally, these conditions—which are entirely up to the individuals involved—should be drafted in advance of a lifelong commitment. However, it's never too late to get down to the "cores."

Nonnegotiable core agreements, once committed to, serve as ultimatums; they're "walking" matters. (See Chapter 9, "Walking.") For that reason, they really do need to be consensual. Any couple who can't agree to the core conditions of their relationship should refer to Chapter 10, "Help." If doing what those pages suggest doesn't result in agreement, perhaps the relationship isn't worth saving. We always have to think carefully about the wisdom of committing to—or trying to preserve—a relationship where our essential needs aren't accepted and valued.

Though on the surface, core agreements may appear a little

heavy, cold, clinical even—clearly, they do have teeth—they're actually an invaluable gift we can share. Like nothing else, such pacts between us lend strength, structure, stamina, and substance to our relationship. Over the life of our love, they'll come to function as the very I-beams of the trust we feel for each other.

BATTLING THE SEVEN OUTLAWS OF LOVE

Though your individual core conditions, and the agreements you forge from them as a couple, are yours alone to design, certain general conditions are recommended. These are intended to shackle the seven outlaws of love:

❶ Infidelity
❷ Sexual acting out
❸ Violence
❹ Lying
❺ Addictions
❻ Extreme self-destructive behaviors
❼ Criminality

Many individuals regard these outlaws as obviously unacceptable and therefore don't think it's necessary to formally agree to disallow them, but it's always preferable to be explicit about such matters.

Core conditions grow out of *what has proven to work*—to both create and sustain vibrant relationships. All the outlaws named above—including, for example, infidelity and violence—are like big gashes in the vessel of a relationship; they typically defy repair. They destroy trust and all hope of ever establishing that particular relationship as an emotional safe zone. Additionally, they stymie the fulfillment of higher-order needs for self-love and emotional intimacy. With the help of core commitments, these outlaws can be barred from any relationship.

Though all seven outlaws are destructive, some are worse than, more common than, and more complicated than the others. We'll take a closer look at how commitments to monogamy and sexual exclusivity (not the same thing!) can restrain two of the worst offenders, and then turn our attention to ways to combat violence (whether manifested in word or deed).

Committing to Monogamy

Monogamy is a matter of personal choice, but it's something that most of us commit to in principle. The rationale for that commitment isn't based only on physical health; it also takes into account—and this is to our credit—emotional well-being. And although we might say that we just "couldn't handle" two sexual relationships (not to mention sharing our beloved with someone else in this most intimate way), we who insist on monogamy are also displaying a healthy regard for our own most human and, incidentally, gender-neutral fears: those of abandonment or rejection, and of being found to be inadequate or unlovable.

While for most people the mere idea of our mate in bed with someone else is disturbing or worse, the act itself is severely traumatic and destabilizing. Indeed, as the sixties taught us, even when both partners agree to an open relationship, that arrangement generally doesn't work. Almost invariably, once one partner acts upon the option, the other, if emotionally honest, takes it as a sign of his or her own "not-enoughness" (if not as an actual betrayal).

The ramifications of multiple partners on the energy of a relationship are equally important. Sexual energy flows between two people like electricity in a circuit. When a third party is introduced, he or she breaks the circuit, diluting—*squandering* even— our own precious sexual energy. Even between partners who are aware of no abandonment buttons or lack of self-love, the energy loss of sexually open relationships precludes emotional depth. There's just no way around it: the highest realms of sexual ecstasy can be experienced only by mates who are bonded on the deepest level of friendship and feeling—and who reserve themselves for each other exclusively.

Committing to Sexual Exclusivity

Beyond monogamy, the sixth Natural Law of Love also encourages us to make a core agreement with regard to sexual exclusivity—that is, an agreement to not interact (read: act out) with other people in a sexual manner. Sexual acting out has caused tremendous confusion and pain for many partners—particularly in our generation, since so many sexual taboos have been lifted—and it continues to be terra incognita for most of us.

A crucial refinement on the notion of monogamy, sexual exclusivity is much more far-reaching than a straightforward agreement not to sleep with another. In fact, it proscribes a wide range of sexualized behaviors and interactions not only *with* others, but also *about* others with one's mate. These include, in the first category, flirting, staring, rubbernecking, and making sexual comments, compliments, and jokes; and in the second, comments to one's mate that demonstrate sexual interest in, excitement about, or titillation by another. Often both categories of behavior are rationalized as acceptable, on the grounds that the offenders "aren't actually doing anything." This is a serious misjudgment, however; for in the sanctity of the love union, these partners are doing something—not only sexually acting out, but also eroding fragile trust.

A core agreement on sexual exclusivity might read as follows: "In honor of the specialness of our sexual chemistry and out of our respect for each other as people, we agree to reserve all our sexual energy for one another; this includes touching, playing, flirting, and all other seductive behaviors with others." At first glance such an agreement, which calls us to refrain from what some might be tempted to call "innocent sexual fun," may seem to be pandering to unreasonable insecurities (petty at best and paranoid at worst). It's not. While the effect of acting out sexually isn't usually as traumatic as that of physical infidelity with another, any form of sexual involvement with a third party—even if that third party is a pornographic image—will likely feel like a betrayal to one's mate.

A core agreement for sexual exclusivity averts such recklessness and heartache and honors the specialness of the connection. Couples are encouraged to define for themselves—as soon as possible—what, beyond standard monogamy, they expect in terms of sexual exclusivity. This can be challenging, because many of us have been shamed for being sexually insecure, possessive, or jealous. We can take advantage of our best-friendship closeness to exercise emotional honesty as we communicate these difficult feelings to each other.

Committing to Emotional Exclusivity

Many of us feel uncomfortable or hurt when our partner maintains an intensely emotional relationship with someone of either gender outside our couple. (Of course, if this third party is a family member, this is an issue of individuation, as discussed in Chapter 2, "Priority.") Though not exactly sexual or romantic in nature, such a relationship can feel like a genuine betrayal of the emotional primacy we have the right to expect with our partner. These sticky dynamics are much more complex than sexual acting out, and we usually require some facilitation to determine whether we're detecting a truly codependent or otherwise inappropriate relationship, or whether it's our own low self-love that ails us. Usually it's a confounding combination of both. The resources listed in Chapter 10, "Help," are strongly recommended for such cases.

More at the Core

Core agreements that proscribe violence, dishonesty (including criminality), and addictions and compulsivity—essentially, all issues of priority—provide an equally stabilizing function in couples. Indeed, such agreements are the "good cops" in our emotional safe zone. Relationships in which outlaw behaviors are tolerated can be true hell on earth—a state none of us deserve to live in. Unfortunately, outlaws figure in the autopsies of many a once-hopeful relationship.

Partners who find such a list of core agreements to be more than they can insist on—or who sense a tendency to minimize or deny the existence of outlaws in their relationship—have a strong need for outside support. Chapter 10, "Help," offers considerable help in this area.

Couples are encouraged to create whatever additional core agreements they need. For some, these might cover areas vital to their sense of individual security—finances, for example, which they might choose to protect in the form of a standard prenuptial agreement. Other partners might craft cores to safeguard cherished personal values and life goals, such as a religious or spiritual orientation or a decision regarding having children. (This sort of core agreement has some overlap with essential compatibilities as defined in Chapter 1, "Chemistry.") We recommend that couples who do want a family also both agree that physical discipline, meaning any nonloving touch, is unacceptable. Couples concerned about spiritual issues might want to agree on the children's religious or spiritual upbringing as well. Expectations regarding caring for aging parents or other relatives for whom either partner is responsible, financially and otherwise, should also be explicitly covered in an agreement. Finally, couples with a history of pathological or compulsive lying, any form of addiction, extreme self-destructive behavior, criminality, or mental illness should draft a core agreement committing to stop the behavior; in addition, ongoing recovery or treatment are crucial for both parties, offering structure as they attempt to rebuild trust

Many couples find that the Ten Natural Laws of Love handle everything. And though the Law of Priority has already asked us to do the work of relationship using a new model, some partners make it easy on themselves by committing to all Ten Natural Laws of Love, in addition to the specific cores recommended in this chapter.

RECOMMENDED CORE AGREEMENTS FOR THE NEW COUPLE

Here is a suggested script for your couple's core agreements, to be modified as you wish:

Inspired by our deep respect and love for each other, and by the preciousness of our chemistry, emotional intimacy, and trust, we [add your names], agree to commit to the following:

Monogamy

Sexual exclusivity [as defined by your couple]

Non-Violence

Honesty

Sobriety in all Forms

Non-Criminality

The Ten Natural Laws of Love

Your couple's additional core agreements then follow.

For example:

A family of at least one child

Parenting education at all developmental levels and outside support when necessary

Anger Management

THE BEDROCK OF OUR EMOTIONAL SAFE ZONE

Though unglamorous perhaps, effective anger management is the bedrock upon which the peace and health of all relationships—including those of a romantic nature—rest. Over time, unmanaged anger caused by buttons and blind spots not only shuts our hearts to each other, but turns our household into a place where angels—and everybody else—fear to tread. Chapter 2,

"Priority," introduced the idea that all feelings—anger not least among them—inevitably find release. If we don't express feelings responsibly using I-statements, we act them out irresponsibly, either directly or indirectly. Our understanding of this distinction is fundamental to our ability to both manage anger and resolve conflict.

Our commitment to anger management signifies a commitment to neither act out nor tolerate the acting out by our mate of any kind of anger. This includes garden-variety anger, rage, resentment, frustration, impatience, irritation, and annoyance, and the contempt cluster of emotions—namely, hatred, scorn, disdain, and contempt. This commitment comes into play when emotional management isn't enough—that is, when one of us acts out *despite our knowledge of the information and skills outlined in Chapter 3—Emotional Intergity.*

Anger management asks that we recommit to the definition and inadmissibility of all forms of acted-out anger. Additionally, it asks that we both agree to use the anger-management tool known as the "time-out" and—if an incident needs further resolution (which it often does)—to hold a "time-in" as soon as possible to determine what course of conflict resolution we should take. (More on this process later.)

Anger management isn't about stifling our anger; it's about taking dominion over it, controlling the impulse to release an explosion of bile or rage the moment our anger button is pushed. Neither is anger management about promising never to act anger out again—that would be absurd. Rather, it's about doing our best. Unfortunately, we're all sitting on veritable powder kegs of anger stored from a lifetime of large and small psychological insults and injuries. Given the destructive potential of these powder kegs, many of us will need to learn how to discharge this surplus safely and appropriately through catharsis, initially with the help of a trained professional. Then, with less raw anger to manage, we won't have to keep a finger in the dike to prevent catastrophe. (The peacemaking section of Chapter 10 provides further suggestions along these lines.)

Still, it's essential that we agree not only on the unacceptability of mismanaged anger—and commit to use a procedure for those times when anger erupts—but also on a common definition, so that together we can name what threatens us. The naming of anger can be challenging, however, because acted-out anger occurs in a seemingly infinite variety of forms, be they passive-aggressive or aggressive-aggressive, verbal or physical. While it's not hard to recognize and label violence, the breaking of objects, and over-the-top verbal abuse as acting out, some of the subtler forms of the latter—such as sarcasm and teasing—can be trickier to nail, especially in the confusion of the moment.

Surely the worst problem is that, like sexual acting out, many forms of acted-out anger are socially acceptable; they're common currency in our homes, schools, and workplaces, and they show up to an alarming (and increasing) degree on radio, television, and the big screen—as entertainment, no less! All this family and cultural conditioning creates tremendous pressure on those of us who are trying to master the distinction between acting out anger and expressing it appropriately. As with sexual acting out, those of us touchy about tolerating the verbal acting out of anger shame ourselves for being too sensitive or unable to take a joke, roll with the punches, or be a good sport. We often end up minimizing or rationalizing the offensive behavior as acceptable—or denying it altogether.

Labeling Our Anger

Though the labeling of acted-out anger is difficult, we owe it to ourselves to master the skill, because it's the first step in managing anger. In fact, vagueness or a lack of consensus at this crucial first step sabotages the entire peacemaking process.

In her book *The Verbally Abusive Relationship*, communication expert Patricia Evans details fifteen categories of verbal abuse.

Not surprisingly, most of them are couched as you-statements and bear the disrespectful tone of an abusive authority figure. Our modified list, some categories of which were mentioned in Chapter 3, follows. You'll notice the list begins with the most direct, overt or *aggressive—aggressive* forms of acted-out anger and proceeds to the most indirect, covert or *passive-aggressive* forms:

1. **Name-calling**: Using vicious, hateful names, names disguised as endearments (such as "My Little Dummy" or "Dingbat") or names a partner has objected to in the past.

2. **Threatening**: Intentionally or unintentionally frightening the other by physical raging (storming, slamming doors, pounding walls and tables, etc.), using obscenities (either directed at partner or not), and making comments that raise partner's worst anxieties. Can be conveyed by both words and tone of voice, gestures, etc. "I wouldn't do that if I were you." "I want a divorce / to be separated." "There are a lot of people out there who'd appreciate me." "Somebody's going to get hurt, and it's not going to be me."

3. **Bullying and Commanding**: Adopting an authoritative, coercive, dominating or disrespectful tone and/or words. Can be psychologically violent, as in "Shut up!" "You're not leaving this house." "Get into the car." The tone of voice makes the following unacceptable: "Give me that remote." "Turn that radio off." "Let's go."

4. **Interrogating**: Delivering a stream of questions in a hostile, intimidating, shaming or imperious way; implying (as in the category of bullying and commanding) that one is in authority. "What time did you get home? Who drove you? How much did you have to drink? What were you wearing?"

5. **Interrupting and Contradicting**: Violating our mate's right to express him- or herself by keeping him or her from being able to speak. Changing the subject, making accusations and counter-accusations, and other tactics aimed at preventing discussion and avoiding divulgence of information. "Do we have to get into that?" "My spending? You've never saved a penny in your life." "Do you expect me to walk on eggshells?"

6. **Accusing and Blaming**: Charging one's partner with inappropriate behavior (either falsely or not) or of breaking an agreement in order to avoid responsibility for one's feelings, actions or a situation in general. "You were supposed to go to the post office." / "Well, you were supposed to pick me up at work." "You're so controlling (or demanding or whatever)." "You never . . ." "You always . . ."

7. **Judging and Criticizing**: Making direct or indirect judgments or criticisms whether through words, tone of voice or non-verbal communication (such as a sneer, raised eyebrow, mocking laugh). Includes character assassination and invalidation or negation of partner's feelings. "You're just like your mother / father my ex-." "I thought you were smarter than that /a good business man."

8. **Sarcasm, Teasing and Joking**: Offering jokes, teasing, or sarcasm at a partner's expense, whether through words, tone of voice or non-verbal communication (such as a sneer, raised eyebrow, mocking laugh). Typical areas of vulnerability for this form of shaming include femininity or masculinity, sexual desirability, intellect, competency or physical appearance. "You're not wearing that out in public, are you?" "You're late. Let me guess? You got lost again." "Looking a little pudgy, aren't we?"

9. **Lying and "Forgetting"**:   Lying about facts or invalidating the reality, experience or memory of one's partner. "That's not the way it happened." "I never did / said that."

    "Forgetting" involves actually not remembering or "getting foggy" on vital details; this is a kind of denial in which a person believes the false information is true. *e.g.*, "I said what?" "When did you hear me say that?" "I don't remember that."

10. **Minimizing, Trivializing and Discounting**:
    Questioning, devaluing or minimizing a partner's experience or perceptions. Attacking a partner's self-esteem by deflating his or her interest and enthusiasm by belittling and shaming comments.   "That didn't really bother you, did it?" " You're making a mountain out of molehill." "He didn't mean any harm when he whistled at you. It was a compliment."

11. **Guilt- or Pity-Tripping**: Manipulating or making oneself pathetic to get our way without asking, these covert, indirect forms always mask rage and an unwillingness to take responsibility for self. "It's beautiful, but I wouldn't have spent that much on myself." "How do you think it makes my mother feel that you don't want to spend the holiday with her?" "I have to do everything around here." "I'll be fine here all alone all weekend." "Don't leave me!"

12. **Psychoanalyzing**: Offering an unsolicited psychological assessment, insight or advice. Always shaming, dominating, attempting to exercise power over. "You're being childish." "You're a codependent." "You have no boundaries." "You need to learn how to say 'no.'" "Boy, do you need therapy!"

13. **Moralizing**, Lecturing, Teaching and Unsolicited Advice: Use of any of these in an intimate relation-

ship. Always involves an authoritarian, shaming or dominating dimension, however subtle. "You shouldn't fraternize with a person like that." "You shouldn't smoke / eat pie / let you gym membership lapse, etc." "Here's how to handle that situation at work."

14. **Nagging and Hen-pecking**: An attempt to dominate, manipulate or control by persistent harassing, scolding, complaining, or urging. "When are you going to take out the trash?. . . Did you remember to take out the trash?. . .Have you forgotten to take out the trash?"

15.}**Withholding, Shutting Down/Out, Silent Treatment** (British: putting other "in Coventry"): Keeping to oneself in order to punish. This type of nonverbal communication is actually emotionally violent and a form of psychological abuse.

Time-Out and Time-In Tools

Once two partners have agreed on the definition of acted-out anger, they need to agree to use the anger-management tool. This tool entails four specific steps.

First, when one partner acts out anger, the other first says, simply, "Ouch!" This is the first, relatively gentle intervention. It signals that a partner is treading on thin ice. If the "ouch" stops the acting out, there's no need to carry on to the second through fourth steps.

Second, if the early-warning "ouch" fails to halt the first partner's acting out, the next step is to say, "Time out!" This is the big gun, to be used only when "ouch" fails. The first partner then stops talking. Period. Midsentence, midword, whatever. Since the ball is always in the court of the one on the receiving end of the anger, it's always his or her responsibility to put the tool into action—and it's always the responsibility of the other partner to cease and desist.

Lest there be any question on this point: everybody hates being timed-out. Everybody. It's extremely frustrating to be at the beginning or in the middle of a cathartic and seemingly justified release of pent-up frustration (or clever but scathing commentary), only to be stopped in our tracks by our mate. To the person timed-out, this rage-buster seems like a rude interruption—an adult-inappropriate, infantilizing gimmick better used by parents with out-of-control kids. That point is well taken. Indeed, most acting out between adults, regardless of our age, is a result of both partners regressing into youngsters—either a pair of neighborhood bullies, or a bully and his or her victim, a much younger child. So this unassuming technique is age-appropriate after all! Be that as it may, respecting a mate's "ouch" or time-out is one of the most emotionally mature acts of self-discipline that we'll ever muster or master. Along with deep listening, it's one of the greatest acts of love.

Third is to choose, together, whether to stop discussing the conflictual topic, stop talking altogether, or leave each other's company. The decision will depend on the severity of the conflict and its potential for escalation. Partners who want to choose the last option but are in a car, in an airplane, or in some other situation that makes leaving impossible can simply refrain from talking. The rub comes if the partner who was interrupted is unwilling to honor the time-out, despite having agreed in principle ahead of time. When that happens it's the responsibility of the person who called the time-out to remove him- or herself from the presence of the other.

Fourth is a "time-in"—an agreed-upon coming-together to discuss how to proceed. This step takes place whenever both parties feel that it's safe to reconvene—that is, when they both trust that they're able to refrain from further acting out. This could be a few minutes after the initial incident, or up to (but not exceeding) twenty-four hours later. If the intervening cool-down period has been enough to dissipate tension, no further resolution is necessary. If, however, one partner is still experiencing residual anger—

which, frankly, is most often the case—both partners will need to decide jointly which of the three conflict-resolution options would be most appropriate: the Path to Peace, the written Path to Peace, or a negotiated agreement (all discussed below).

Conflict Resolution:

CREATING A LASTING PEACE

Whereas the purpose of anger management is to minimize the possibility of hurting each other with our acted-out anger, the purpose of conflict resolution is to heal fractures and get back to trust and love, which are always waiting. For if emotions are like the weather, then love is like the sun: it's always out, even if clouds or the earth itself blocks our view. The so-called negative feelings, like bad weather, simply lead us to forget the fact of love's omnipresence.

Weather happens. And in couples, conflict happens. Who among us hasn't felt anger hit us like a hurricane, sadness fall like rain, fear blanket us like freezing snow, and depression—the numbing of all feelings—descend like the dark night? Who among us hasn't despaired that love would be forever lost?

The New Couple conflict-resolution tools—*the Path to Peace*, in spoken and written forms, and *negotiated agreements*—are exceptionally powerful ways to bring love back into the life of your couple, especially when used in tandem with the time-out.

Path to Peace

The Path to Peace is a safe, effective method for resolving most interpersonal conflicts. The only time this tool isn't suitable is when we're addressing anger related to core conditions or agreements. (For more on resolving core issues, see Chapter 10, "Help.")

As we've already noted, the Path to Peace works well as a conflict-resolution tool following a time-out (if during the time-in that follows, we determine together that it's the appropriate method of conflict resolution). But that's only a fraction of its usefulness. We can use the Path any time either of us feels angry, upset, or "separate" from the other—as long as neither feels at risk for further acting out.

Does this mean that all heat and tension have to have totally subsided before we can use the Path to Peace? No—but both partners must feel sufficiently in control of the initial anger to use the Path in good faith and to the letter. It doesn't even matter if we don't yet know exactly why we're upset or what feelings are involved. The Path will help clarify these issues.

The Triangle Test: Assessing Path-to-Peace Readiness

One simple way to find out if we're ready for a successful trip up the Path to Peace is the Triangle Test, inspired by the work of Eric Berne, founder of Transactional Analysis.

Assume that we each have three main parts or subpersonalities, each positioned at a corner of a triangle. At the top is "the Adult," at one bottom corner is "the Child," and at the other bottom corner is "the Critic."

The Adult—our "preferred" self—is wise, rational, loving, emotionally literate, and honest. The Child is creative, spontaneous, and playful, but also codependent, rebellious, vulnerable, and easily guilt-tripped, shamed, frightened, and intimidated. The Critic is tyrannical, judgmental, perfectionistic, disrespectful, bullying, shaming, and guilt-tripping. Whenever we communicate, one of these selves is "holding the mike."

Only one of these three selves is emotionally mature enough to use the Path to Peace, and that's the Adult. The other two always act out; they're the ones that got us into conflict in the first place. Before taking a turn going up the Path, we need to ask ourselves, "Who's got the mike? Where am I on the triangle?" (Although it can be tempting, we need to refrain from asking each other these questions, because to do so could actually constitute acted-out anger – not to mention allowing the Critic to talk!) Having the Adult at the mike doesn't necessarily mean that we're not angry, only that we're committed to expressing our anger in a healthy way—using I-statements.

The Path to Peace itself is an adaptation of an anger-management technique introduced by relationship expert Barbara De Angelis in her book, *How to Make Love All the Time*. It uses a special listing of emotions (and quasi-emotions). The main difference between that listing and our listing of emotions in Chapter 3 is that, unlike our earlier discussion, the Path to Peace excludes all unhealthy emotions (toxic guilt and shame as well as the contempt cluster), which are never appropriate to use with this tool. The Path also includes understanding and responsibility, which, though not technically emotions, are still necessary to express to our partner in order for us to arrive at real peace.

Here's what the Path to Peace looks like:

- Empathy step: Understanding, gratitude, joy, appreciation, compassion, admiration, and love

- Ownership step: Healthy guilt, healthy shame and responsibility

- Fear step: Fear, anxiety and worry

- Sadness step: Sadness, disappointment and despair

- Anger step: Anger, resentment, frustration, annoyance and irritation

As we deliberately make our way up the Path to Peace, we address each emotion in turn. Sometimes only one of us is angry; in that case, only one of us needs to use the Path. Still, it might happen that something our mate says on his or her way up the Path will trigger us into new anger or resentment, in which case we simply ask for our own turn when he or she is finished. Specific issues and conflicts, however, usually involve two people; in these cases, we alternate as many turns up the Path as necessary until we've both returned to a state of love and trust.

A "trip" up the Path takes about ten minutes. When we're ready to use this tool, we need to go (with this book in hand) to a peaceful place by ourselves where we'll have no interruptions whatsoever. As we sit facing each other, the partner with the most heat goes first.

We can resolve only one issue per trip up the Path to Peace, and it must be a single, specific incident in historical time. For example, we can go up the Path to resolve the specific incident of our mate making plans to meet friends for dinner on the upcoming weekend without consulting us first, but we can't use the Path to resolve the general issue of our mate's pattern of not consulting us. The second issue isn't specific enough. And though it may be true that a pattern exists, generalizing—saying, "You *always*. . ." or "You *never*. . ."—almost always creates more discord. Generalizing involves a degree of measurement-taking that can't be absolutely accurate (and thus can't be absolutely fair). Furthermore, anger causes us to distort issues, again endangering fairness. For these reasons, single incidents in historical time can be resolved far more successfully than general issues can using the Path to Peace.

When we go up the Path to Peace, the one expressing anger is "the Speaker"; the other person is "the Listener." Beginning at the bottom of the Path on the anger step, the Speaker formulates a brief I-statement using any of the feelings listed there (see above). For example, "I feel frustrated that you forgot to help our son with his homework when I was traveling—and he failed his test." He or she then communicates that I-statement to the Listener. It's essential that these I-statements be brief—mere sound bites—because the Listener needs to be able to repeat them back verbatim. This repetition both assures the Speaker that the Listener is really listening and gives the Listener a chance to experience what it's like to be in the other's moccasins.

Neither the Speaker nor the Listener should ever abuse this precious peacemaking tool by acting out while working up it. In other words, both partners need to keep the Child and the Critic under wraps! It's essential, and only fair, that the Speaker use a respectful, nonintimidating, nonshaming—yes, Adult—tone of voice. If this is impossible, the Speaker is still too angry to use the Path to Peace properly. It's always the Listener's job to determine if this is the case and to end the Path by calling a time-out.

After the first I-statement is communicated by the Speaker, the Listener takes a deep breath and repeats back exactly what he or she just heard, using precisely the same words. These are the only words uttered by the Listener, with two possible exceptions: asking the Speaker to repeat the previous I-statement, and (if these statements are running too long to remember) reminding the Speaker to use sound bites.

On the anger step, at the bottom of the Path to Peace, the Speaker is limited to a total of five I-statements. (Communicating anger is a delicate business, and we don't want to overwhelm the Listener.) On all the other steps, however, the Speaker can deliver as many I-statements as the heart dictates, as long as the minimum—one from each step—is met, *no exceptions.*

Feelings on certain steps may be easily accessible, while those on others may take a bit of effort to contact. This is normal: as the Law of Emotional Integrity has taught us, we inevitably have emotional blind spots. And yet we have to make the effort to get in touch with even the difficult feelings. Trying to skip a step to avoid particular feelings doesn't work, because every level of emotional truth must be found—and communicated—in order for the Path to Peace to do its magic. With a little patience, we can surprise ourselves with the richness of our own emotional landscape.

If the Listener simply can't control him- or herself and lapses into sighing, rolling the eyes, repeating the Speaker's statements in a sarcastic or mocking tone of voice, or showing impatience, the Speaker must end the Path by calling a time-out. These acting-out behaviors are a big-time abuse of the Path to Peace.

Once we've completed the anger step of the Path to Peace, we continue together to the sadness and fear steps (all of this taking only moments). The Speaker can make as many I-statements as desired, and the Listener repeats back precisely what he or she hears.

At the ownership step, the Speaker (still using I-statements) has the opportunity to plunge into quintessential Adult territory—and the heart of peacemaking—by "owning" something. Ideally, this means acknowledging how he or she contributed to the initial conflict. For example, "I feel guilty that I gave you the silent treatment when I found out that you didn't help our son before his test." If the Speaker is unable to identify any such responsibility in a particular incident, it's enough to recall and communicate having committed a similar "crime." One example of such peripheral ownership is, "I'm guilty of having forgotten his parent-teacher conference last semester." As always, the Listener repeats verbatim what was said.

At the empathy step, the Speaker does the best he or she can to reveal some understanding or appreciation of the Listener with regard to the incident. For instance, "I understand that you were swamped with two parents' jobs while I was away." The Speaker can be exhaustive in this effort; at this step, the more I-statements, the merrier.

If the Speaker can't find anything to say on either the ownership or the empathy steps, the anger step may well have been incomplete. In this case, the Speaker is to go back to the beginning of the Path and work his or her way up again.

A SAMPLE PATH TO PEACE

Let's look at this peacemaking tool in action. The conflict that prompted this particular trip up the Path occurred when Bob made some weekend dinner plans with friends without consulting Carol:

Anger Step (first communication)

speaker (Carol): I'm frustrated that you didn't ask me before you made plans with Ted and Alice for Saturday night!

listener (Bob): Repeats Speaker's words verbatim: I'm frustrated that you didn't ask me before you made plans with Ted and Alice for Saturday night!

Anger Step (second communication)

speaker (Carol): I resent that you didn't first check in with me at work before committing to our friends.

listener (Bob): Repeats verbatim

Sadness Step (first communication)

speaker (Carol): I'm disappointed that it apparently didn't occur to you that I might want to spend the evening alone with you.

listener (Bob): Repeats verbatim

Sadness Step (second communication)

speaker (Carol): I'm hurt that you didn't take into consideration that we've been out with others every weekend for the last month.

listener (Bob): Repeats verbatim

Fear Step (first communication)

speaker (Carol): I worry that you'll do it again.

listener (Bob): Repeats verbatim

Fear Step (second communication)
speaker (Carol): I'm afraid that you were unable to say no to them.
listener (Bob): Repeats verbatim

Fear Step (third communication)
speaker (Carol): I'm anxious that you'll expect me to do the canceling if we decide not to go.
listener (Bob): Repeats verbatim

Ownership Step (first communication)
speaker (Carol): I take responsibility for not clearly telling you that I miss private weekend time with you.
listener (Bob): Repeats verbatim

Ownership Step (second communication)
speaker (Carol): I feel guilty that I signed you up for dinner with my parents last month before I consulted with you.
listener (Bob): Repeats verbatim

Ownership Step (third communication)
speaker (Carol): I'm ashamed that I yelled at you when you told me what you'd done.
listener (Bob): Repeats verbatim

Empathy Step (first communication)
speaker (Carol): I understand that Ted put you on the spot and pressured you when he invited us.
listener (Bob): Repeats verbatim

Empathy Step (second communication)
speaker (Carol): I feel compassion for your difficulty saying no to pushy people. I know you're working on it,

and I have difficulty too.
listener (Bob): Repeats verbatim

Empathy Step (third communication)
speaker (Carol): I really appreciate your letting me go up
the Path to Peace and listening so patiently.
listener (Bob): Repeats verbatim

Very often a single trip up the Path to Peace doesn't resolve a
conflict entirely. In our sample case, for example, Bob might now
feel relieved about the initial incident but be angry about something Carol said while going up the Path. In order to work
through that anger, he would need a turn up the Path as Speaker.

Important Path to Peace Pointers

Not surprisingly, most Path to Peace issues revolve around various forms of acting out (especially of anger), the breaking of
agreements, and the lack of needed agreements. (The type of
agreement called for in Bob and Carol's case—called a *negotiable
agreement*—will be covered in the next section.) The first three
steps up the Path to Peace provide an opportunity to fully express
our so-called negative feelings to our mate while maintaining our
emotional safe zone. Since those negative feelings are going to
come out one way or another—that old law of emotional physics
again!—we use the Path to guarantee that our anger, sadness, and
fear can be released without casualties.

The couple above did a good job of keeping their focus on a
single issue and refraining from second-guessing, ascribing
motives to, and psychoanalyzing each other's behavior on the
anger and sadness steps. Instead of saying, "I'm angry that you're
codependent with our friends," the first Speaker stuck to describing the behavior and her reaction to it: "I resent that you didn't
first check in with me at work before committing to our friends."

The Speaker waited on the motivational issue until the fear step and then expressed, *as a fear*, a guess about what might have been behind her partner's behavior: "I'm afraid that you were unable to say no to them." This was a wise move on her part, since it kept her from making assumptions about her mate—assumptions that not only would have been disrespectful, but might also have resulted in another collapse of trust.

The ownership step is based on a crucial (and for some, radical) assumption: that *without exception, every conflict takes two.* The corollary of that assumption is that each of us bears a degree of responsibility that must, in the name of justice and resolution, be "owned." As we noted earlier, the ownership expressed in the Path to Peace can reflect either responsibility specific to the current conflict (as when the first Speaker said, "I take responsibility for not clearly telling you that I miss private weekend time with you") or similar culpability from the past (as when the first Speaker said, "I feel guilty that I signed you up for dinner with my parents last month before I consulted with you").

The everyone-is-guilty assumption doesn't imply that we both start every argument jointly, or that one of us doesn't hurt the other more in a particular argument—although such comparisons are fodder for another fight and are thus not recommended. Rather, it maintains that in the day-to-day conflicts that occur between two intimates, each so-called victim has colluded in the offense in some way (however well concealed). This collusion could be the simple act of not calling a time-out before feeling seriously transgressed, or it could be not insisting on making an agreement about an item of great importance.

This revolutionary premise underlying the ownership step also borrows from the universal principle of our shared humanity—the fact that all of us possess a variety of facets, including "shadow" sides, and that we're all capable, on some level, of acting out. It's that understanding that opens our hearts as we ascend the ownership step. And with open hearts, we refuse to take a high-and-mighty, pot-calling-the-kettle-black position, even though we might blame our beloved for a particular problem.

We choose instead—and what a powerful choice!—to build an "empathic bridge" back to our beloved, letting him or her know that we've "been there and done that" too, or that we recognize we weren't exactly a saint in this instance either. The noblest element of the ownership step in particular (and the Path to Peace in general)—and one of its greatest benefits—is that it moves partners through the need to be right (or to have been "wronged") and over and over again helps us transcend together what's literally a microcosmic representation of the dynamics of war.

The Written Path to Peace

We always have the right to decide that the Path to Peace isn't working when it seems that one or both of us simply can't get the mike into the hands of our Adult self. At these times, it's best to take another time-out on the subject and agree to give it another go when we both feel ready. If this still doesn't work to our mutual satisfaction—that is, we don't yet feel that we can completely trust each other on the issue in conflict—we may need some hands-on coaching (see the "Peacemaking" section in Chapter 10), but it would be better to first try the written Path to Peace technique described below. If this flops too, our issue is probably "too heavy" for the Path, meaning that a major button, blind spot, or unresolved trauma is most likely being triggered. Since couples are inherently egalitarian, it's a good bet that this is happening for both partners at the same time. Since it's a shared issue, the negotiable agreements covered in the next section may be able to restore sanity to the debate.

The written Path to Peace is just like the spoken one, except—you guessed it—it's in writing. In the peace and privacy afforded by this exercise, we often discover more emotions on each step than we would have verbally. For that reason, it's okay to make up to ten I-statements on the anger step in this form of the Path.

(However, all the other instructions given for the spoken Path to Peace apply to the written version as well.) To get the greatest benefit, we need to read the letter aloud to our partner as soon after writing as we can, going slowly enough to allow him or her to repeat each I-statement verbatim. (Remember: if this is one of those double-trouble topics where we profoundly disconnect, then it's time for Chapter 10, "Help.")

Sometimes, after successfully resolving a difficult conflict with a written Path to Peace, we can glean even greater insight by excavating the issue more deeply using a Special Session. As we've seen, these gems are better than open discussion, since they provide the structure we need to ensure that we both have our say. Again, though, a Special Session wouldn't be appropriate in cases where our anger isn't fully dissipated. Remember that the Listener reserves the right to call a time out and terminate the Session if he or she detects any reignition of hostilities. Then it's either back to the bottom of the Path to Peace or on to Chapter 10.

Negotiable Agreements

LITTLE PACTS FOR *PAX*

Once the core agreements are in place, never to be questioned again, the sixth Natural Law of Love proposes that couples adopt a second kind of agreement: negotiables. If at this point the New Couple is starting to look like the *Rule* Couple, let us reassure you that, by definition, this couldn't be. For agreements aren't rules, though some partners may argue this point. Whereas rules are imposed by an authority figure onto a subordinate, agreements are tools of fairness and democracy, created together by and for peers. And if we can't hope for a successful relationship without core agreements, then we'll never be able to extricate ourselves from the power struggle without *negotiable* agreements.

It's a golden rule of peacemaking that the heart must be lightened before the head can be effectively engaged. In a state of unresolved anger, we're incapable of thinking clearly. Therefore, the drafting of negotiables (like any planning or problem-solving) must never be attempted before all our feelings have been completely resolved on both sides via the Path to Peace. Skipping this step can result in an ineffectual or unsatisfactory agreement, and it risks forcing us to revisit the initial argument, necessitating yet another time-out. Therefore, we must follow the peacemaking process to the letter, first managing anger via a time-out and then melting hard feelings using the Path to Peace. Only then, if the situation calls for it—that is, if we think we're likely to stumble over the same issue in the future—do we go on to create a negotiable agreement, the last step in the peacemaking process.

To fashion a negotiable agreement, we begin by identifying our needs. This is best done as early in the relationship as possible. Some needs we're obviously already aware of, such as not wanting people to smoke in the house; others will become clear as we spend more time with each other, such as the desire for time on the shared computer. Once the needs have been identified, the next step is to communicate these needs to one another as directly and specifically as possible. Then, after discussion, we can create simple agreements.

Standards of tidiness are good candidates for negotiable agreements, because housekeeping is an issue for most couples. When we're single, we can be as obsessive as we want, labeling and dating everything in the freezer if that makes us happy, or we can indulge in slovenliness, collecting as many inches of dust as we please. But cohabitation means shared space. To make our home a haven, we may have no healthy choice but to discuss what we consider fair and get the details into an agreement. We might agree on the following, for example: "To the very best of our ability, we agree to leave the kitchen the way we found it."

Of infinite variety, negotiable agreements cover every conflictual corner of our relationship not already handled by our "cores." They can help bring balance to areas of inequality, including the sexist ruts we often get into regarding household chores. Parenting chores can also be negotiated. When both parents have to get up early for work, they might work out something like the following for their nighttime obligations: "We agree that whatever the problem, we'll alternate wake-up duty for the kids."

Together we design as many—or as few—negotiable agreements as we want, on an as-needed basis *throughout the life of our love*. Some negotiables concern our couple directly—like where vacations will be spent, how money will be generated, whether in-laws will live in, which parenting style we'll adopt, even how much (if any) contact with former partners we'll feel comfortable with. Others are highly individualistic, like those respecting the desire for further education or the need for silence, private time, a special diet, or a smoke-free environment.

When we find ourselves poles apart on an issue, we need to enter into negotiation before we can reach agreement. Not as fancy as it may sound, negotiation is a straightforward process in which one of us proposes, and then the other counter-proposes (and so on, back and forth), until we reach a scenario we both feel comfortable with. Both couple-oriented and individualistic negotiables can involve some serious wheeling and dealing, and they may need to be reassessed and possibly renegotiated down the line.

Becoming proficient at creating negotiable agreements draws on the full battery of our developing New Couple skills. Not only will we need the time-out and the Path to Peace (in spoken or written form), but we'll need to avail ourselves of deep listening, emotional awareness, emotional fluency, and emotional honesty. On top of all that, we'll need as much self-knowledge—especially about our buttons and blind spots—as we can summon.

If this seems daunting, rest assured: the ability to identify needs and work to meet them is a natural extension of everything we've learned and practiced up until this point. And as we practice still more, we'll find that the more we're in touch with, and expressive about, our emotional reality, the more obvious our own needs will be; in fact, some can just be skimmed off the surface. There will be times, though, when we'll find it difficult to know our own boundaries, understand what's fair for us, set limits, or articulate what we need. At those times, we'll benefit from the insights shared in Chapter 7, "Self-Love," and in Chapter 10, "Help."

There will be times, too, when we break our agreements—often even the very ones that we ourselves campaigned hardest for. Ironically, the beauty is often in the breaking. For when we break a negotiable agreement, we have to make amends (a process that, incidentally, often involves another explicit agreement!).

Amends-Making:

WHEN "I'M SORRY" DOESN'T CUT IT

Amends-making can be almost magical in its ability to put things right again between us. An integral part of the peacemaking process, it involves the giving of a small "favor" or gesture thought up by the "offended" partner—anything from a foot massage to taking over dish-duty for a night to a bouquet of flowers to the handling of an irksome errand. The only requirement is that whatever we decide upon has to satisfy the recipient and be considered fair by the one making amends. In order to meet this requirement, we sometimes have to engage in a mini-negotiation.

Though such a gesture may appear strictly symbolic (and therefore flimsy), its power to melt away residual animosity shouldn't be underestimated. While a straight apology may be music to our ears, sometimes it feels dismissive, not to mention insincere. Amends, with their tangible offering of apology, run circles around "I'm sorry."

Making amends brings resolution to a particular breach of agreement, but it's not necessarily the end of the issue. We need to remember that negotiable agreements are subject to renegotiation: we don't need to live forever with what we created on the first go-round if it doesn't accurately reflect what both of us want and need. Furthermore, a breach of a negotiable agreement, unlike that of a core agreement, isn't a walking matter. If a certain negotiable agreement is broken repeatedly, however, and we're unable to renegotiate it to both partners' satisfaction, we may need to check out Chapter 10.

New Solutions to Age-Old Problems:

THE PEACEMAKING PROCESS IN SUMMARY

The traditional couple must have heaved a giant sigh of relief when television recognized the entertainment value of reality and beamed Archie and Edith Bunker into their living room. For years, they'd been miserably trying to match the plastic personas of Ward and June Cleaver. The fact is traditional couples didn't have the benefit of what we might call peacemaking "technology." They had to rely on conventional wisdom, which strongly urged lovemates to turn the other cheek, forgive and forget, let the issue go, or kiss (or have sex) and make up. Sweet, swift, and certainly well-intentioned as such counsel may have been, it just plain didn't work; in fact, by modern psychological standards, it was patently avoidant. Anger and conflict don't go away with a peck on the cheek, be it figurative or otherwise.

Most curious of all, perhaps, was the adage warning partners never to go to bed angry. Given that anger is energy and can be neither created nor destroyed, being true to this advice would have required a couple to pull many an all-nighter. Among the most potent emotions, anger always needs to be fully acknowledged and healed, and this often takes time. Additionally, if anger has been acted out, getting back to deep trust requires further work— namely, a real protocol to resolve both partners' feelings and the issue at hand, plus a plan to give anger proper and safe egress next time it threatens to erupt.

Conventional marriage vows were perhaps intended to function as core agreements, and they did point partners in the right direction. But because they didn't tell people how to get or stay there, they were inordinately difficult to keep. When the inevitable conflicts arose, goodwill, patience, and willpower stood in for anger management, and "talking problems over when everyone's calm"—a state that's rare indeed—epitomized conventional conflict resolution. Even the concept of win-win was unknown in traditional relationships. Historically, arguments and grim tolerance supplanted healthy negotiation, and announcements stood in for negotiable agreements. All in all, this left mates no choice but to take unfairness in stride. An unprioritized marriage, neglected higher-order needs, few (if any) emotional or listening skills, and entrenched inequalities all conspired to lock many of them in a perpetual power struggle. This is why, for all their attempts to create harmony, our predecessors deserve our utmost regard and compassion.

They deserve our thanks as well, because we've learned a great deal from their hard lessons. Today we can put the peacemaking trio—core agreements, anger management and conflict resolution (which includes negotiable agreements and amends-making)—to work right from the get-go. We desperately need these established ways to keep or restore the peace, because every single conflict and incident of acted-out anger (unless acknowledged and healed) can put a crack—perhaps invisible, perhaps dramatic—in the trust of our couple and cause a dissipation of our precious chemistry. While we can handle a high percentage of these anger episodes with a simple "ouch" or time-out, the other peacemaking skills are also primary to the New Couple.

The truth is problems actually benefit couples. Over time, if we handle them with even a modicum of skill, they take the fulfillment of our higher-order needs for emotional intimacy and self-love to new heights. Because every time we say "ouch" or call a time-out on our mate—or honor this simple anger-management technique when it's used on us—we're making sure that neither one of us gets hurt. Every time we resolve an issue using the Path to Peace, we don't merely avoid a grudge (and potentially a lot worse); we simultaneously compound our trust in ourselves and each other. That's because this enlightened tool facilitates a thorough and safe ventilation of the full range of our feelings, thereby bringing about healing for both of us individually and for the relationship itself.

Whether core or negotiable, every agreement we create stabilizes our relationship. Each time we respect a negotiable agreement, we introduce more sanity into our power struggle and assure a more rapid advance into co-creativity. Negotiables are powerful—even in the breaking. For there's nothing like the feeling when our partner acknowledges that he or she has blown it and offers to make amends. The experience of trust being mended through that process is almost palpable.

Since both cores and negotiables are designed by the couple alone (with the help of a few recommendations from this book), they represent an amalgam of our basic needs. This summary of needs can be priceless if our mission in life isn't already apparent. For the more in touch we are with what's basic to us as individuals, the more our big direction can come clear. In fact, our core and negotiable agreements form a tapestry, a beautiful creation unique to our couple alone.

With our peacemaking technology in place this sixth Natural Law of Love invites us to adopt:

- When anger is acted out in your couple, the partner who recognizes the anger first says "ouch" or calls a time-out. Then both of you decide which of the following options is appropriate:

- Stop discussing the conflictual topic.

- Leave each other's company.

- Refrain from talking at all.

131

WHAT'S THE STATE OF YOUR UNION?

- When you're both in Adult mode, as determined by the Triangle Test, you then take a time-in to jointly decide whether to resolve conflict via a Path to Peace, a written Path to Peace, or, if there's no remaining anger, a negotiable agreement.

- Finally, you move on to the conflict-resolution method chosen, doing one of the following (or all three in sequence):

- Work your way up the Path to Peace. (If either of you is unable to remain in Adult mode and follow the format, try again later. If the tool fails again, proceed to the written Path to Peace.)

- Draft and share a written Path to Peace.

- Create a negotiable agreement.

THE KEY TO PEACEMAKING

Keeping the peace and maintaining an emotional safe zone in your couple is the key to the sixth Natural Law of Love.

This means …

Clarifying your core conditions individually and creating core agreements.

Acknowledging the unacceptability of acted-out anger in any form.

Learning to manage your anger using the time-out tool.

Learning to resolve conflict using the Path to Peace tool.

Learning the skill of creating negotiable agreements and making amends when those agreements are broken.

SELF-LOVE

AFFIRM A COMMITMENT
TO PERSONAL HEALTH

Self-love is a confusing topic for couples. The old thinking has long been that to enjoy a healthy relationship, we need to put aside the preoccupation with—and therefore love of—ourselves, and shift this focus onto another.

In this traditional perspective, the love of self and the love of other have been seen as somewhat mutually exclusive. The new thinking is that to love another, we need to be psychologically whole and love ourselves first.

Though it obviously calls for a balance, the newer thinking is definitely closer to the mark. Self-love is now firmly established among the psychological community as a higher-order need that all adults must honor, whether we find ourselves in a relationship or not. And many "other-loving" behaviors, long conventionally held as the very models of how to treat a partner, are now being recognized as subtly self-sacrificial and codependent. But—and here's the rub—the love of, and by, another person is also essential for healthy adulthood.

Certainly, two already fully self-loving individuals would make an ideal couple. *But it's a long road to buddhahood.* More often than not, our higher-order need for emotional intimacy compels us to form relationships long before we're "completed." Hence, either limping or striding, we all enter into romantic unions suffering to some extent from a deficit of self-love. Fortunately, coupledom's grand design helps unfinished adults heal from the slings and arrows of our past. When based on love, it's a two-sided enterprise in which we build a healthy relationship with ourselves and with our beloved at the same time. In fact, these two projects are not only interdependent, they're synergistic.

To some of us, the term "self-love" might seem too strong, too much like self-centeredness, egocentricity. By contrast, self-esteem seems more socially acceptable, only halfway toward the outrageous idea of outright love of self. The seventh Natural Law of Love prefers *self-love* (both as term and as concept) because it's much more direct, and we all have a long way to go to learn that there's nothing shameful about truly loving ourselves. In fact, all selfishness, greed, self-centeredness, egocentricity, egomania, and self-obsession—subsets of what psychologists call narcissism—are manifestations of the extreme opposite—that is, harrowingly low self-love.

What It Is, What It's Not

Self-love is our deep personal conviction that, when the music stops, we're absolutely okay. Self-love enables us to take for granted that we're essentially lovable and worthwhile—in and of ourselves and regardless of whatever roles, titles, or successes we may (or may not) enjoy. High self-love leads us to trust our feelings and intuition automatically. Because it reinforces our sense of personal rights, it helps us say no, set limits, stick up for ourselves, and keep ourselves safe both physically and emotionally as a natural response to any kind of threat. In fact, the ability to use the time-out, an anger-management tool discussed in the previous chapter, demonstrates this component of high self-regard. Self-love lends us much more than the power to care for ourselves as individuals in every way we can conceive; it empowers us to thrive. It leads us to our mission in life and enables us to experience true emotional intimacy with another. Perhaps most important, this incompletely understood but essential brand of love endows us with dignity, giving us the ability, whatever the circumstances, to hold our heads high.

It's important to note that the self-love of this seventh Natural Law of Love is distinct from the narcissistic "love" that popular culture would have us buy into. The latter is conditional, dependent on external factors such as money, looks, credentials, and talent. While in our hearts we all know that conditional love is absurd, on some level we have trouble believing that we're worth the oxygen we consume if we can't hit a golf ball like Tiger Woods, look and act like Michelle Pfeiffer, think like Stephen Hawking, or write a check like Bill Gates.

And yet, as we busy ourselves chasing our tails, the props of conditional self-love always remain ephemeral. Even those born with (or, through hard work, are able to acquire) such externals as wealth still live in terror of losing them—unless they love themselves solidly at the center. Despite our sincerest efforts to control conditional self-love, it ebbs and flows with every failure and success, tossing us about through all the vicissitudes of life.

In comparison, *unconditional* love is constant and therefore affords peace. It's true bliss when we can manage to achieve it, but it comes long and hard. We arrive in adulthood with our tanks very low. We're burdened by a host of buttons and blind spots, by toxic guilt and shame and their accompanying fear of abandonment. Unable to love and take care of ourselves completely, and to honor our own feelings, personal rights, and intuition absolutely, we attempt to compensate. We try to bolster our conditional self-love with a variety of impressive externals. Inevitably, we also end up, to varying degrees, seeking from others—be they mates, children, parents, other relatives, bosses, colleagues, or friends—the love and validation we can't give to ourselves.

Why Low Self-Love?

It's no mystery that humanity's almost universally low self-love comes primarily from the circumstances of nurture—in other words, from the raising that parents do. We're born with high self-love, every one of us. It's only our interaction with others (especially our earliest caregivers) that impairs its proper development. Far from being an indictment of our parents, though, this is a simple fact of the evolutionary process: as we advance as a species, each generation becomes more educated and able to refine what went before. Though our parents inherited many ideas on the subject of childrearing, they had nowhere near the information, tools, emotional support, or opportunities for healing that they needed in order to be what child psychologists call "good-enough" parents. In fact, in their day, the words "self-esteem" and "self-love" were rarely used.

Our parents and other crucial early caregivers often had little idea how to validate our feelings or deeply listen to our ideas and concerns. Nor were they informed about the nature of emotional trauma, not to mention instructed on how to help young ones recover when something traumatic did happen. In fact, we now know that many of the old-fashioned techniques our own parents used to rear and discipline us were themselves traumatic—and thus the source of much of the low self-love that partners suffer today.

For instance, when a child is instructed repeatedly to be a "big boy" and not cry, he becomes traumatically shamed about the expression of sadness and grief; when children are spanked, especially by the very people who represent safety and protection, the violence of the nonloving touch is traumatic. If such acts are accompanied by words such as "This hurts me more than it hurts you," they add a layer of toxic guilt, making the child feel responsible not only for his own beating, but also for hurting the parent.

So everyone's guilty but no one's to blame: our parents were themselves victims of unenlightened childrearing practices and plagued by their own unresolved trauma and deficit self-love.

Despite their most steadfast and heartfelt efforts—their genuine desire to do well by us—they visited their trauma and low self-love upon us as well. All in all, evolutionary status and cultural conditioning had the last word: there was simply no way our parents could have been raised to enjoy unconditional self-love or could have raised us to have it.

Just as it's only in relationship with others that our self-love is stunted, so it's only in relationship with others that it can be restored. Naturally, as we grow up, friends, teachers, parents of friends, colleagues—even family members, including parents!—all substantially aid us in mending certain areas of low self-love. There will always remain impaired areas that fail to develop properly. For while almost nothing can keep us from maturing physically, unmet needs arrest our development emotionally. Though as adults we look all grown up, our exterior rarely tells the truth about our interior. Those aspects of our emotional self that correspond to each unmet psychological need have been unable to mature.

In Defense of Inner Children

Psychologists use such terms as "inner child" and "irrational self" to label the invisible and "unfinished" interior that each adult exterior conceals. By whatever name we know it, this inscrutable dimension of our humanity must not be theoretically dismissed. As all of us who have been in love know, it does exist—*and it has the power to sabotage even the most auspicious matches.* Furthermore, it's much fairer to ascribe difficult behaviors and attitudes to a part of us than to condemn ourselves—or our partners—as immature in our entirety, which is what many people who lack an inner-child understanding tend to do. Without a grasp—and appreciation—of the inner child, we struggle to develop compassion for ourselves and our mates and to raise our self-love.

Often in a state of semi-slumber, our inner-child selves are awaiting the arrival of nothing less than a new parent. This person need not be a literal, full-fledged mother or father figure, of course.

137

A lover will do just as well—so it seems to the inner child—to complete whatever our parents left undone when they raised us. The child hope is that this someone will at least be able to validate emotions, listen deeply, and show interest in our gifts—the basics of good-enough parenting. If there was even greater lack or trauma in childhood, the younger parts of us might even be seeking a mate who can provide for us at the level of lower-order needs—that is, food, shelter, and a basic sense of physical safety.

Some of our inner-child issues are all too familiar to us, while others remain alien. Our metaphorical child selves are capable of lying low for years on end—until, that is, they're triggered by a relationship. Then, sometimes to our great embarrassment, they make a surprise appearance. The determination of these inner selves must not be underestimated: one way or another, they busily push their little agendas. Still, it's never our partners' responsibility to finish this parenting job—even if, out of the kindness of their heart, they genuinely want to. Anyway, they've already done a lot to help us raise our self-love merely by facilitating the emergence of our inner-child selves into the light of day. It's our responsibility—and ours alone—to pick up for ourselves where our parents left off.

Transference:

EMOTIONAL HANGOVER FROM THE PAST, BLIND SPOT IN THE PRESENT

Transference, the stuffy-sounding phenomenon whereby we "transfer" the role of primary caregiver or sibling onto another person, is inevitable in couples. Identifying and labeling this phenomenon was one of Sigmund Freud's greatest contributions to psychology, although he limited his work with transference to the relationship between therapist and client. But the truth is transference happens in all relationships all the time. And it's most profound in those relationships possessing a dimension of romance. In the intimacy of the sexual-emotional connection, our child self is reminded of the first bond of its lifetime—the one it had with its parents or parent surrogates. This memory link results in a radical case of mistaken identity. And though for many lovers this is hard to believe, we encourage that mistaken identity by unconsciously picking mates who remind us, in positive and negative ways, of the people who raised us or were around us when we were little.

It's not surprising, then, that in those moments when our partners exhibit negative traits that echo our past, we experience a kind of *déjà vu*. On some occasions we wonder when we've felt this unpleasant sensation before; at other times we know exactly. The catalyst provided by the reappearance of the old feeling provides us a platinum opportunity to sew up that old business and heal once and for all. In fact, without those irksome features of our mate to dramatically bring to the surface what's unfinished, we could go a lifetime suffering low-grade, chronic deficit self-love. That's why, as outrageous as it sounds, a part of us (wise, but beyond awareness) actually chooses lovers because of the specific kinds of headaches they'll bring—and the cure they'll force us take.

Naturally, for the system to work optimally, our mate can't function solely as a catalyst. He or she also needs to act as our favorite catch-basin—in other words, to be committed to being there to help us catch and heal the old problem and support us through the process of growing our self-love. It takes two people equally committed to this enterprise to get the process of transforming transferences off the ground. Exactly how a couple can do this is detailed below.

Transference and the Stages of Relationship

As unsexy as it may sound, all partners enter the first stage of relationship part adult, part well-disguised kid unconsciously seeking a good-enough mother and father. Naturally, at this early and ecstatic point, we're spared most signs of our lover's low self-love; for we are, after all (at least figuratively), under the influence. Chemistry has been discovered and is being celebrated, and though transference is definitely in play, it's mainly positive—*an idealizing distortion of our partner.* That's because the unfolding mystery of a fresh relationship brings out the best in both partners; in fact, it leads each mate to perform many of the functions children need from their parents. For example, we typically hang on each other's every word, fuss over each other's every feeling, and exhibit our most loving and nurturing adult behaviors.

Eventually, however, transference is destined to go from positive to negative—*to a devaluing distortion of our partner.* Somewhere between two weeks and two years after our relationship starts—whatever the duration of our particular intoxication stage—the personas drop, we begin to get used to each other, and that wonderful deep listener and emotional confidant of not too long ago becomes a little less available. There's no denying it: this most precious person now has "behaviors," buttons, and blind spots—all, incidentally, precisely correlated to areas of deficit self-love; and sadly, we two now have "issues."

Though the adult part of us expects some eventual change in the personality of our mate, the child experiences the onset of the second phase of relationship as an about-face and a betrayal. "Where's this person who was supposed to be here for me?" he or she laments. Additionally, when our partner's new behaviors unconsciously remind us of parental shortcomings or childhood traumas—*and there will inevitably be occasions when they do*—things get much worse: big buttons get pushed, blind spots catalyzed, and painful areas of low self-love triggered. Indeed, frequently the emotional flashbacks can be so intense for us that our adult self loses ground, becoming subsumed by our inner child's emotional memory and distorted perception.

The 80/20 Principle of Transference

It's not that the power struggle somehow triggers these transferential distortions. On the contrary, it's transference that precipitates the power struggle. In fact, this by-product of low self-love is likewise to blame for almost all the irrational, extreme, out-of-control—in short, childlike and bullying—behaviors that necessitate the use of anger-management technology.

As monumental as this crisis of mistaken identity is, affecting every single romantic partnership, the majority of us in love have never even heard about transference. As our relationships unravel, we unwittingly and indirectly blame each other for what happened to us as kids, despite the fact that (very unscientifically) *as much as eighty percent of the emotional juice of each couple conflict is leakage from the mysterious reservoirs of stored feelings from childhood.* Only the remaining twenty percent actually pertains to the contemporary situation. This is called the eighty/twenty principle of transference.

The Hard Underbelly of Transference:
Parental Idealization

If transference really is couple enemy number one, why is it such a mystery to the general public? The first reason is that with relationship education virtually nonexistent until recently, most couples are simply uninformed: the severe effects of transference on couple health have yet to be made part of today's popular consciousness. The second reason is that transference functions like a blind spot. As Chapter 3, "Emotional Integrity," explains in detail, most of us skim the surface of our emotions like feather-light bugs on a lake; below churn dark, mysterious waters composed, in the main, of archaic feelings associated with our parents and siblings. This deeper emotional reality is difficult for many mates to contact, mainly because of a seriously underestimated, but monumentally important, childhood need—that is, the need to idealize our parents or early caregivers.

When we were tiny, these people weren't just bigger than we were, they were bigger than life. And they had to be, for we were dependent on them for our very survival. That's why as very young children we felt the need to perceive them as perfect, in every way up to the task of raising us. Still, well-intentioned and special though they were, they occasionally strayed from the mark and failed to meet some of our core emotional needs.

When such a fall from grace did occur—say, for example, our mother ignored us instead of empathizing with some upset, big or little—we had two choices: we could acknowledge our mother's failing (shattering the idealization that made sense of a scary world), or we could rationalize the failing away. Because the first option was simply unthinkable, choosing the second option was a matter of great psychological urgency. Though feelings of disappointment, shock, anger, or fear did arise in response to our mother's behavior, we bypassed them, denying to ourselves intellectually that the lapse in appropriate care ever happened. Responding to the developmental need to keep thinking of our parents as heroes, we then blamed our disappointment (or other emotion) on our innocent little selves.

Regrettably, it takes very few instances of maintaining the parental idealization at our own expense to cause us a lot of trouble. These experiences are the genesis of our epidemic inability to completely love ourselves, the toxic guilt that distorts our sense of responsibility, the toxic shame that convinces us we're not lovable, and the fear of abandonment that results.

Small wonder, then, that most of us enter partnership more or less unindividuated and stuck in the mire of parental idealization. Other factors also collude to candy-coat our early histories. First, we often simply can't recall our early traumas, because the events that had the greatest impact on us occurred while we were in the cradle, crib, and preschool. Second, though some people do naturally have an accurate grasp of the early events of their lives (sometimes having worked hard to achieve it), many partners share a very understandable human propensity to screen out memories that are unpleasant.

But whether our early hard times are truly forgotten or are simply screened out, they remain a blind spot. Tucked away, they still have great power, convincing us that even huge reactions to small incidents in our couple are strictly the fault of our mate. Unless our early traumas and the idealization that disguises them can be "unpacked," they have the potential to trap us forever in the power struggle and impede the growth of our self-love.

The Voyage Out:
Overcoming Transference

So how can we keep transference from eating our love alive? Better yet, how can we turn this massive blind spot into an opportunity to build trust and raise both partners' self-love?

The first step is the identification of transferential issues in our couple. That step is relatively straightforward, but it's not always easy. *Any button, blind spot, or issue that requires the use of a time-out indicates transference.* The emotional charge behind these elements is a giveaway. In addition, a high percentage of couple conflicts that don't need anger-management technology also belong in this category—specifically, those we're unable to resolve to both partners' satisfaction using the Path to Peace. The key question in identifying transference is always, "Have I ever felt this way before? If so, with whom, and when?" Usually we have to step back a little to answer this question, but once we do, we can flesh out the picture of our family relations, avoid displacing old feelings onto our partner, and have compassion for the child we once were.

Many of us, whether we realize it or not, go through our love relationships still trying to please, reject, avoid, or rebel against the idealized members of our families-of-origin. As we saw in Chapter 2, this failure to individuate—to become psychological peers with our family members—prevents us from prioritizing our couple. But the problem isn't irreversible. If we're able to spot transference, pin down the connection with the past, and then transform that connection through the process of individuation, we can focus with new honesty and clarity on our current relationship. Though it often takes some digging and courage, "owning" transference is

143

a watershed both for the individual and for the couple, since it's fundamental to our ability to individuate from our families-of-origin and to maintain our relationship as an emotional safe zone.

When we try to recapture the relevant old information behind a reaction that we recognize as transferential, at first there might be only a thread (as is often the case when we try to remember dreams). But if we grab that thread like the tail of a tiger, we might be able to pull the whole scenario back into view. Lovemates can be excellent sounding boards for each other in this effort, but it takes time. Putting together a coherent picture of earlier relationships with the prime players in our childhood—a picture devoid of the distortions of idealization, devaluation or fantasy—happens issue by difficult issue, not in a single fireside chat or even a single New Couple Session. But the effort is gratifying: when we succeed at even the first step in the process—remembering who "made us feel this way" in the first place—both partners generally feel a tremendous relief. Sometimes that step alone is enough to resolve the issue and lift our self-love a notch.

Occasionally, in attempting to trace back a particular feeling, some of us will have zero recall. In these instances, it's important to be willing to accept, at least in theory, that we may be masking events that are too painful to remember. This kind of forgetting can indicate unresolved emotional trauma and the need for outside assistance. (See also Chapter 10, "Help.")

The next step in healing a transferential issue comes under the jurisdiction of the Law of Emotional Integrity. It involves taking responsibility for all the original emotions now unfairly reappearing in our love life. Often it's necessary that we actually work through these messy emotions. There are many ways to do this, *but it's never necessary to confront parents—or other primary caregivers—directly.* (Therefore, it makes no difference whether they're living or deceased.)

How does taking responsibility for these old emotions work? First we hold a Special Session with our partner in which to safely talk about the incident or relationship that's being triggered by present circumstances, keeping the focus off our partner's twenty percent of the issue and on the transferred eighty percent. Sometimes this is enough to interrupt the transference. If more work is needed, another simple and often highly effective method for working through transference is to write a no-holds-barred letter expressing as many negative feelings as we possibly can. This, of course, we never send; in fact, once the letter is good and complete, we might even choose to destroy it. If we've been taught other forms of catharsis, such as pounding on or yelling into a pillow or provoking our own tears with sad music, these too can be helpful. In cases where such exercises fail to neutralize the transference and the accompanying emotional charge—be it anger, sadness, or fear—Chapter 10, "Help," (Any reader who's frightened by the above suggestions shouldn't attempt to try them but should instead go directly to the guidance in Chapter 10.)

When we identify transferential issues and undertake to resolve the early hurts at their roots, we're taking care of the eighty percent that has nothing to do with today. What's left is the other twenty percent of the issue—that which does pertain to our current relationship. This can be dealt with using the Path to Peace, sometimes with the help of negotiated agreements, as taught in Chapter 6, "Peacemaking." But remember that until a given transferential issue is acknowledged and at least brought forward for resolution, the Path to Peace won't work.

BRIEF INSTRUCTIONS FOR WORKING THROUGH TRANSFERENCE

The following review summarizes the process for working through transference:

- First you need to recognize that you're "in transference." The telltale signs are *any* button, blind spot, or issue that repeatedly requires a time-out -or- *any* button, blind spot, or issue that's too heavy for the Path to Peace

🌿 Once you suspect transference, ask yourself these questions:

Have I ever felt this way before?
If so, with whom, and when?

🌿 To break the transference, do as many of the following as seem appropriate:

🌿 Hold a Special Session with your partner to discuss the incident or relationship that's being triggered.

🌿 Write a letter packed with negative emotions that you never send to the person who first upset you

🌿 Use other emotion-releasing techniques that you've been taught.

Refer to "Help" Chapter 10 for additional guidance

Self-Love Then and Now

As we noted earlier, to the traditional couple the concept of self-love would have been virtually alien. Surely today's ideal of self-love, which concentrates on validating our own feelings and intuition and pursuing personal dreams, would look worse the further back we went into the less-enlightened past. In fact, it would become indistinguishable from base selfishness. And to the unenlightened, childhood experiences would be seen as largely irrelevant to adulthood, not to mention couplehood. How people "turned out" both as individuals and as spouses would have been seen as mainly a matter of character.

Even today, among our own parents' generation—people for whom self-esteem is still a new idea—self-love might seem too bold a goal. Our parents, and the couples that came before them, had no inkling about idealization and transference, no concept of how these deadly dynamics entrapped them in the power struggle of their own relationships. They knew nothing of any of the developmental stages of relationship; in fact, they didn't realize that there were stages! And if someone had raised the notion of the "resolved" power struggle, known as co-creativity, it would have been dismissed as a fairy tale. Like communities of old anticipating the Black Death before antibiotics, many among those who raised us—and those who raised them—could do nothing but anticipate the souring of love's sweetness as "what happens." Most tragic, perhaps, was what they were left to privately conclude: that they'd failed, either as spouses or in their selection of a mate.

While certain forms of selflessness undoubtedly had a civilizing effect on marriage, selflessness has long outgrown its usefulness. Under no circumstances is it healthy, or even workable in a relationship, to deprioritize our mental or physical well-being or dishonor our emotions or dreams. Ignoring childhood trauma is equally unhealthy. If we find ourselves stuck in an idealization of our early caregivers, unwilling to be what we perceive as disloyal to them, we will unavoidably transfer our denied negative feelings onto our beloved.

Transference is a wily beast even in the hands of a self-aware New Couple, because intimate relationships always bring up our deepest self-love wounds. For this reason, many people find self-love the most challenging and redemptive of all the Natural Laws of Love. Even couples who have been basking for years in the co-creativity stage of their relationship still occasionally encounter old (and sometimes even new) areas of unresolved emotional trauma—issues that make themselves known through those telltale buttons and blind spots. Even having cracked colossal idealizations, shed seemingly fossilized family roles, and worked through maddening transferences, there are still times when each partner seems to mutate into the worst caricature of the other's brother, sister, mother, or father—and the transference-busting force of the Law of Self-Love has to be applied anew.

While it's important not to set the bar too high, the intention to apply this law represents a heroic journey for modern couples.

For such an endeavor always involves a foray into the unknown or forgotten, a metaphorical return home, in order to set right what's been left amiss. Using our transferences to grow ourselves up—and become true adults vis-à-vis every member of our family—enables us to polish the jagged edges of our individual pasts and clear the way for our future together.

Along with peacemaking, emotional integrity, and deep listening, self-love serves as a cornerstone of our emotional safe zone. The beauty of owning our transferences—a process necessary to self-love—is that we get to the absolute source of our upsets rather than taking them out on each other. This ownership drains much of the negative emotional drama from our relationship by radically reducing acting out and acting in. Emotional intimacy can't help but blossom in the honesty of that environment. The foundation of growing self-love then supports us to develop talents, discover buried dreams, and achieve our mission in life. With transference vaporizing and the power struggle retreating, we can be model emotional intimates, primed for our next great adventure—and doing our bit to coax modern love out of the Dark Ages.

THE KEY TO SELF-LOVE

Committing to raise your self-love by learning to do the following is the key to the seventh Natural Law of Love:

❧ Accept and validate your own emotions, ideas, intuition, and talents.

❧ Stick up for yourself.

❧ Recognize and heal transferences within the relationship.

OUR LIFE'S TRUE CALLING

Would that we each had the blessing of a "signal" childhood moment, announcing definitively the nature of our life's true calling. To the great frustration of many of us, however, this isn't how it unfolds. Our ultimate place in the world often remains a mystery through our school days and on into adulthood—sometimes even well into our parenting years.

Still, veiled or revealed, mission in life is a higher-order need: it's integral to our ability to love ourselves and, by extension—this is the revolutionary part—to keep our New Couple chemistry vibrant. If we don't devote our working hours to what satisfies our soul, we die on the vine.

That's why a commitment to discover and fulfill our own mission in life—*and to support our partner in the same*—has to be one of the Ten Natural Laws of Love. As we find out who we really are as individuals, all our relationships grow and flourish. The benefits of that process accrue not just to ourselves and to the world, but to our beloved as well. And if we're foundering in life, unsure of our mission, there are few places as well suited to helping us find our big direction as the creative crucible—and emotional safe zone—of our most intimate relationship. Mission in life (along with, for some of us, the joy of our growing children) is the essence, the melody, the very heart of our final phase of relationship, co-creativity.

Mission is what gives meaning to our lives. More than a good job or even a prestigious career, it's our ultimate fantasy work, as only we can define it—our "job from heaven." Always unique, this mission—this *calling*, if you will—tends to shape itself to our needs, growing into ever truer versions of itself as it incorporates the unique palette of aptitudes that we were born with. When we commit to work that not only challenges and satisfies us but also helps, however modestly, to turn our world around, we feed our self-love; and perhaps nothing is more deeply fulfilling.

It's important that those of us who don't yet feel called be patient with ourselves. If we lack Mozart's luck—he's one who saw his future as a young child—the discovery and fulfillment of our life's mission could well span our lifetime. And yet however off the mark each little job we undertake may look or feel, hindsight invariably teaches us that everything we've ever done has served as a stepping-stone. Furthermore, as we enhance our self-love, new gifts and talents have a tendency to emerge. We are, after all, works in progress, and we owe it to ourselves to enjoy the journey's twists, U-turns, and occasional detours.

Whatever our dream arenas, the Law of Mission in Life is an invitation that challenges each couple to commit two sets of talent in a tangible way to the good of the world. This doesn't mean sacrificing a nice home, creature comforts, and fun for humanity's sake. In the first place, because true work doesn't represent a zero-sum option, it needn't compete with our material objectives. Furthermore, as anyone who's manifesting his or her personal vision will attest, doing what we were put on earth to do is fun; if we're not enjoying our work, we haven't yet found our mission.

A genuine mission in life is so central to the definition of *human being* that Abraham Maslow, father of humanistic psychology, claimed that all of us have not only the right, but also the need, to pursue a mission. In fact, the Maslovian concept of "self-actualization"—of doing our best and highest work—crowns his famous "hierarchy of needs." The good news is that there's something that each of us can excel at. Harvard University's Howard Gardner proposes that there are seven ways of being "smart"—verbal, mathematical, musical, spatial, kinesthetic, interpersonal, and intrapersonal—and that everyone possesses at least one (if not a combination of several) of these intelligences.

For some of us, the concept of pursuing a mission might seem too highbrow or stressful. Maybe we see the ideal life as retiring at forty off a lottery ticket. Those who've researched the subject of happiness beg to differ; they're enthusiastic life-purpose proponents. Chief among them, Professor Mihaly Csikszentmihalyi, author of *Flow: The Psychology of Optimal Experience*, informs even the most inveterate leisure lizards among us that doing nothing, or doing uninspired work—even with lots of money—will eventually make us miserable. Professor Csikszentmihalyi also asserts that because we're all multitalented, capable of varied tasks, the more pistons we fire in a day's work, the happier and more mentally healthy we'll be. This too supports the view that finding our mission in life—and doing it—is where we're headed as human beings and what it takes to make us happy.

What's good for the lone individual in our era is also crucial for us as romantic partners. For if we ignore the question of why we as individuals were put on planet earth, our souls sicken, and that sickness inevitably infects all our relationships.

Mission Vulnerable:

BIG-PICTURE CHALLENGES

Earth-shattering and thrilling as a calling should be to each one of us, the mission-in-life imperative has barely penetrated society's conventional wisdom. Personal mission has yet to become an ideal of education, and thus we continue to counsel our young people to go for "good jobs" (meaning those that promise the highest incomes), ignoring their natural talents and passions. Given this failure to embrace the higher-order need of mission in life as essential to the well-being of individuals, we can hardly expect mission to be honored as crucial to the health of couples. Even many relationship experts overlook the primacy of dual missions.

Let's take a closer look at three of the major challenges to mission in life: socioeconomic factors, a lack of partner support, and self-limiting beliefs.

Socioeconomics: The System That Stifles

With society so slow on the uptake, mission in life, like self-love and emotional intimacy, is clearly extremely vulnerable: if it's not ignored entirely, it's generally crushed by the pressures of life. Just as socioeconomic factors are often stacked against those of us who choose parenthood, making it exceedingly difficult to be fair in the assignment of roles and responsibilities, the rigidity of the workaday world also negatively affects our ability to be fair to each other—and ourselves—when it comes to pursuing our vocational calling. Some of us are just plain scared that we can't afford to do work that really excites us. On the contrary: we can't afford not to.

For those of us who have the nerve to head down the road toward our mission and then decide we want children, the choices get even more complicated. If one or both of our missions entail financial risks, which many do during the early research phase, the very security of our new family can be jeopardized. Wisely, few couples play these odds. Instead, some solve the dilemma by putting one or both missions on hold. While this is pragmatic and appropriate in the short-term, it poses risk of another kind: that with one leg up, we'll fall off the horse. We may find ourselves locked into dual breadwinner ruts for more than two decades, until the kids are out of college. By the time we feel free to put purpose over practicality, our passions look like pipe dreams.

The belief that we can't fight the system often overwhelms us. For that reason, it's one of the greatest challenges to mission in life. But we can fight it, with determination and a bit of creative planning and financing.

Intimate Saboteurs: Partners Off the Path

No wonder nothing short of a Natural Law of Love, enshrining two missions in life as part of our vision for healthy relationship, would suffice to guarantee that our Big Assignments not go down the drain. For it's perversely true that our very dependence on each other for support automatically magnifies our power to sabotage each other. Indeed, the second biggest challenge to mission in life, after socioeconomics, lurks in the intimacy of our romantic union. If tuning into, and then heeding, our vocational calling can be daunting to us as individuals, imagine trying to accomplish it if our one and only isn't on the bandwagon. When a partner doesn't believe in mission in life as a concept—that is, as a higher-order (and therefore nonoptional) adult need—and doesn't actively support the process of its discovery and fulfillment, then the job of our dreams can end up a nightmare—or worse, nonexistent. In either case, our relationship will inevitably suffer.

Internal Saboteurs: Beliefs That Kill

Unquestionably, partners often hurl monkey wrenches into each other's master plans—with varying degrees of success. Yet spite rarely lies behind our attempts to refute the logic and potential for joy promised by mission in life. Rather, these attempts are due to often outrageously self-limiting beliefs, either conscious or unconscious, that are fueled by low self-love and the trance of tradition.

There's no shortage of mission-killing myths, and most are commonly accepted. Take these three:

- There can be only one mission per marriage.
- Both partners can't have great jobs if they also have kids.
- People can't make enough money doing something they love to support a family.

What these myths have in common is fear, an emotion that can attach itself to anything challenging. For perhaps a majority of us, the fear of being unable to provide adequately for our children has hardened into the almost unassailable belief that at least one of us must choose between family and mission. We think about the difficulty of maintaining two missions and decide that it would be impossible, easily garnering abundant evidence for our sad conclusion. We come to believe that we have no choice but to put in workaholic hours, even at a job we intensely dislike, just to foot the bills.

If these reigning beliefs aren't enough to discourage us all forever, there are plenty more to annihilate ambitions for our next lifetime, too. Other skeptical songs we might be tempted to sing include "It's pure pie in the sky," "Marriage alone is enough (for personal fulfillment)," "You can't win for losing (especially if you tried once and got burned)," "Money and status fulfill," "My mission is to be a good wife and mother," "My purpose is to be a provider," "Exciting work is selfish," and "The seat of my pants are on the seat of my chair." Hummed *sotto voce* under all of these is the anthem of low self-love: "I don't deserve to have a mission in life." Not only is each of the above a lie, but they're also lethal to love (as is any conviction that precludes both of us from finding out and then living out who we really are). Thanks to such traditional tapes, millions of us—including many who see themselves as modern and emancipated—can't begin to imagine the richness of life that's possible as a dual-mission pair.

The Householding-versus-Mission Dilemma

Anthropologist and myth-master Joseph Campbell—a champion

of personal mission—lovingly entreated his public television viewers to "follow their bliss." We're sorry to say, though we can do so with relative certitude, that the majority of Homo sapiens who have died since the inception of the species have died with their bliss unattained. Though the idea of vocational calling wasn't wholly unfamiliar to our parents' generation, people weren't generally expected to give their gifts for either the actualization of the self or the betterment of the planet.

To be sure, there have always been a few people drawn in a special way to their work—people who have felt a calling to the arts, medicine, science, teaching, law, politics, the religious life, or other professions—and they've generally been highly respected. But what is it that sets these committed, successful people apart? Barbara Sher, a pioneer in the field of life-work identification, calls what makes or breaks any person's mission "the right circumstances," and she insists that these are available to us all.

Because mission wasn't part of the average couple's reality in days past, they could rarely recognize or take advantage of "the right circumstances" in which to incubate their life dreams. If, by chance, one partner of the traditional team did feel a tug in the direction of self-discovery, he or she would most likely have been yanked back into line—into mediocrity—by the wrong circumstances, especially the prevailing myths regarding mission in life.

Out of the many myths still active today that deny the need for and validity of personal mission, none has endured longer, or had a greater effect, than the traditional myth that householding constitutes a couple's main mission. The pressure of centuries of post-Industrial Revolution, supposedly biology-based gender inequalities forced men of yesterday to take on the out-of-home job, though that work typically had little to do with his passions or gifts. Women's professional aptitudes and aspirations likewise received little attention, unless they fell within the role of supporting the husband.

In conjunction with the dedicated-worker-and-family-leader

male role and the good-wife female role, the procreative purpose was paramount for traditional adults. Thus our parents and grandparents were also plugged into the roles of male provider and female nurturer. Society so valued these roles that everything was subordinated to the needs of the children, including both partners' dreams (if they had any). Dads exchanged heart for dollars in the most lucrative jobs they could find, locking their genuine interests out in the garage or in their daydreams, or abandoning them completely. Many of these men ended up in middle or old age regretful about past choices and panicked about their mortality. The real tragedy? Unlike women's traditional mission, which included the many gratifications of mothering, men's mission wasn't even about fathering. Instead of enjoying the pleasure of close relationships with their children, our fathers were made to focus on bankrolling our mothers and us.

Whether they wore blue or white collars, traditional fathers risked mild to severe symptoms when continually oppressed in the daily grind of ungratifying work. The lucky ones suffered the rather average rat-race anxieties, along with a sense of purposelessness or isolation. Others suffered nervous breakdowns, substance and behavioral addictions, and heart conditions. Such awful but common side effects, rooted in deficit self-love, tore at the fabric of the traditional couple. Worse yet, dissatisfied breadwinners role-modeled disaffection to their boys. And though we speak of it in the past tense here, the male family-for-mission tradeoff is still pervasive today.

As for mothers, Western and Eastern civilizations have long mythologized childrearing as the adult female's natural and principal vocation. For several decades, however, this traditional premise has been disputed around the world. Indeed, educated and uneducated stay-at-home mothers alike often complain of a sense of purposelessness not unlike the cog-in-the-wheel discontent expressed by their traditional male counterparts. And problems of purposelessness only escalate once the children are grown: the empty-nest syndrome is another unhappy consequence of the attempt to elevate motherhood alone into a mission in life.

Clearly, raising children isn't enough for women today. (Indeed, studies have long indicated that those with the highest self-esteem enjoy both family and career.) Nor is it enough to work at "any old thing" strictly to earn the highest wage possible (often minimum wage), as men do. In fact, many mothers who work for the paycheck only thoroughly resent the fact that they can't be at home. While not having the choice to be at-home moms causes much of this bitterness, what's most devastating is that *the work itself is joyless*.

Unquestionably, the myth of the happy householder has been tragic for the spirit of scores of traditional partners—and continues to be so today. Still, the parenting-versus-mission dilemma was—and is—paradoxical because, after all, raising children is the ultimate grow-ourselves-up experience. Not only can it make us wise, but it can also throw open within us doors of compassion that we might not otherwise have known existed. And because higher purpose always has to do with the betterment of humanity, householding (which centers on the betterment of our own youngsters) has the potential to dramatically aid us in the discovery of that purpose.

Making Our Dreams Happen

So what's the mutually self-actualizing couple like? Who might be exemplars of this New Couple ideal? The pharaonic couples of ancient Egypt, positioned shoulder to shoulder, heads held high, seem to represent the dual-mission dyad, at least in effigy. Rather than looking in opposite directions as "distanced" couples do, or losing themselves in each other's eyes as "enmeshed" couples do, renderings of the early Nile monarchs look straight ahead at a seemingly unified goal somewhere on the horizon. A beautiful and inspiring archetype.

But how can we make *two* dreams come true at the same time, without sacrificing the integrity of our relationship or the family? How can we avoid competing against each other, feeling threatened by our partner's obligations and successes, and stranding our children in daycare? How, in short, can we keep our families together and our wits about us with two major construction projects going up simultaneously? Well, it's not easy: *manifesting two missions in life can be the most complicated enterprise of our partnership.* Probably nothing short of a time- and emotional-management miracle on both our parts will actually do.

Nevertheless, a profusion of innovative employment and childcare practices, such as flextime, job-sharing, family care, and virtual and home offices, prove that solutions to the socioeconomic obstacles to mission exist. As financial expert and visionary Robert Kiyosaki says, "It's never about money, it's about creativity"—and only low self-love could convince us otherwise. All couples have a potentially infinite supply of creativity, and it's just as well, because any combination of two missions challenges both members of the New Couple to pull off an ingenious and dexterous balancing act. Still, it can and—for the sake of our love and our kids—must be done.

Increasing numbers of can-do couples, with and without children, provide ample living proof that it's possible. Despite the odds, these New Couples have successfully managed to hitch themselves, side by side, to their stars. And more often than not, they're pulling it off without privileged background, prodigious talent, or divine guidance. Instead, they're daring to create *within their relationship* the right circumstances in which each partner can incubate his and her dreams—and make them happen.

Certainly, the Ten Natural Laws of Love create ideal circumstances to launch two missions. These laws help guarantee that we don't stop loving each other, put the health of the relationship on hold, or forget that accomplishing our individual missions is part of that health in the first place. The Ten Natural Laws of Love support us in maintaining our best-friendship status, so that (unlike rivals) we can act as each other's most trusted advisor and confidant. If there's a tendency toward workaholism, they remind us to check and balance each other.

The eighth Natural Law of Love helps modern mates cultivate an awareness of conventional vocation-annihilating beliefs and a determination not to be run by them. For example, New Couples don't buy into the idea that socioeconomics have them beat at the starting gate. Nor do they surrender to the other common lies: that they must choose true work or true love or children; that they have no talent and deserve no professional fulfillment; that there's room in a family for only one career; that making money doing what one loves is oxymoronic; or that "having it all" is too much for two people to juggle.

What's more, when those among us committed to this eighth Natural Law of Love find ourselves temporarily encumbered—as many of us do—by impossibility thinking, we're open to getting some help. The same is true when we simply don't know what on earth we're meant to do. Thank goodness, today there are many new methods to help us move through such confusion.

The Dream Session

Discovering the right vocation is as momentous as finding a soulmate; and while both processes require that we follow the dictates of our heart, the identification and implementation of mission typically takes more work. As we've seen, it's an unfolding, creative process that's often rocky. Even after we think we're headed in the right direction, one or the other (or both) of us may feel stuck on the "what," "what next," or "how to." These are critical junctures, and the support we provide each other can make the difference between success and failure. Though support can take many forms, the Dream Session is the most effective and loving way we know of to assist each other in building our dreams.

Dream Sessions are just like Special Sessions except that they focus on the broad topic of our evolving purpose in life. Since Sessions are never interactive, each Speaker needs to keep him- or herself on track. The following questions help direct the broad brushstrokes of discovering and refining our mission:

- What am I doing when I'm most "in flow"?

- What am I doing when I'm feeling optimally joyful or most like my true, empowered self?

- What activities engross me so much that I lose track of time?

- If I had a magic wand, what (down to the detail) would my average workday look like? Where would I be? Would I be alone or with others? Who would these others be?

- How would I spend my life if I didn't have to worry about making money?

- Whose life do I envy? (No matter how out of reach or glamorous the careers of those we idolize might seem, they can serve as divining rods for our own bliss and for the ultimate harmony of our couple.)

Dream Sessions can be very energizing. We may do dozens over the life of our relationship, as the sands of our dual missions shift, each Session revealing further insight into our missions and our relationship. If we already know (or are engaged in a stage of) our life-work but find ourselves confused about logistics, Dream Sessions can help us determine what research we need to conduct on our own and what issues we should brainstorm and devise action-plans for with the help of our partner. This multipronged strategy can help us break through our confusion.

Identifying the Problem

Often our mission-in-life issues come disguised as something else. A man who feels obliged to stay in a stifling job because his wife put him through school to earn his degree, for example, might not recognize that his mission-blocking issue is actually one of individuation. Though he assumes he's responding to pressure from his wife to stay glued to his desk, the real pressure comes from his father, who takes every chance he gets to boast about his son "the professional." He has continued his father-pleasing behavior out of toxic guilt—an inappropriate feeling of responsibility—for so long that it's nearly snuffed out any sense of what excites him. In his case, identifying the problem will likely be harder than solving it. Once a "diagnosis" is made—namely, ailing mission—he can conduct Dream Sessions with his wife to help him explore his true direction.

Likewise, a woman who graduated from college with plans to change the world and got battered for her efforts—as she was battered by her family-of-origin for every attempt to pull herself out of their poverty and negativity—may find herself, a decade later, convinced that she has no dreams left. Describing herself as "realistic," she opts out of what could have been truly worthy work for the "success" she can depend on as she moves up the career ladder in retail. The negativity, self-reproach, and even self-destructiveness she feels is so fierce that it's threatening her recent marriage. One dashed dreamer can easily sink a whole couple, unless denial, bitterness, and limited thinking can be reframed as symptoms of past hurts. She may want to explore her perspective with the help of a professional before undertaking Dream Sessions with her husband.

Unearthing a Treasure Trove

Helping uncover the brilliant truth about each other can be an awesome event for a New Couple. When we meet, at least one of us might still be raw material, a block of marble yet to be hewn. Not unlike Michelangelo, when we're able to see in our lover the angel yet to be carved from the stone, we can help set it free.

Take the internationally known entrepreneur, an expert at making money, who took a workshop expecting to improve his moneymaking capabilities and discovered something even more gratifying instead—something that capitalized on other, as yet unharnessed talents: he found that he was good at helping heal others of what he called "poverty consciousness." He found that teaching others how to discover their life's purpose and create wealth for themselves fulfilled a "burning urge."

Loving his work, he was troubled that his realtor wife did work that failed to excite her. Intuiting that her obscured mission would eventually pose a threat to their relationship, he vowed not to rest until that mission was revealed and realized. He spoke with such enthusiasm about his own fulfillment at work that his wife was soon inspired to follow in his tracks. In three short years, they had together emancipated her "inner entrepreneur." She's now hard at work on a financial empowerment adult-ed curriculum for women.

Many husbands in young, single-career couples today put pressure on their wives to "do something." "She needs to stay busy; she'll get bored at home," they might say. These guys are half right: while certainly "staying busy" isn't the point, and on its own doesn't dignify anyone, no partner can neglect mission without detrimental consequences.

It takes a lot of emotional maturity to dedicate ourselves not only to our own dreams but also to those of our partner. But if we help each other identify who we really are and support each other in never giving up, we'll discover that together we can go down the golden road of mission in life with far more economy, potency, and fun than we can alone. This is the essence of the synergistic potential of the New Couple and the eighth Natural Law of Love.

A Shared Mission

To our utmost surprise—this is your authors speaking now—following our bliss as individuals led us to each other, and almost immediately to a shared mission. Though we were fortunate to have been introduced to the concept of mission in life before we met, the struggle to find its truest expression took years; in fact, it continues today. During our initial wrestling with this issue, as individuals before we knew each other, unfinished family-of-origin emotional business contributed to our confusion. The decision to attend graduate school, where we met, was the mission-in-life turning point for each of us: we took major career and financial risks in committing ourselves to a new direction based on what gave us the most joy.

How did we reach that turning point? At precisely the same time in our lives, we had both entered a period of crisis that went beyond career to identity—what we recognize today as pre-mission existential angst. Though Seana had always recognized her gift for communication, she was never satisfied with her "success." After years as an editor, copywriter, and marketing executive, she decided that the thing she most wanted to sell people on was their own unlimited potential. Maurice, like his partner-to-be, had long been aware of his passion for interpersonal communication of the deepest kind, and he felt a strange incompleteness with his work as a musician. He finally realized that his greatest joy, and true mission, lay in work that involved both healing and teaching.

During our first months together, our dreams and ambitions revealed themselves to be uncannily alike. Hiking the California foothills, we spun out visions of traveling in Asia and plying our psychological skills in the international arena (though how we'd manage all this we didn't know). At the time, with graduate-school loans mounting, we could scarcely afford our own wedding. How could we have predicted the financial windfall that would come our way six months after we'd exchanged vows? Funded by that windfall, we traveled the world as we'd dreamed—twelve countries in as many months. How could we have foreseen the mysterious forces at work when, in Kathmandu, we encountered a Southeast Asian businessman who eventually paved the way for us to establish a private practice in Singapore—also part of our dream? Goethe's famous quote came ringingly true for us: "Whatever you can do, or dream you can, begin it. Boldness has genius, power and magic in it. Begin it now." We would amend it, however: *Begin it now, and nurture it as a couple.*

Eighteen years later, our mission in life is to work as a couple to help other couples both create solid platinum partnerships and support each other to manifest their grandest dreams. We do this via writing, public speaking, individual psychotherapy, couple counseling and relationship training, and New Couple seminars. This book is one of many expressions of our mission in life. It wasn't until we dared to commit ourselves to the health of our couple—and kept fine-tuning the directions we got from our hearts—that we were able to begin actualizing our life-work. People often ask how we can tolerate so much time together. So far, it still brings us joy.

Having It All

Undoubtedly, laying the groundwork for a gratifying life together takes commitment, coordination, and an investment of time and (for most of us) education. Leaping before we look might be exciting, and sometimes even necessary, but it can create untold complications and stress, especially if we have kids. Still, our children deserve to grow up in the glow of two fulfilled parents, each of whom has quality time to spend with them. They need us both to "get a life"—for their own health as well as for ours. Obviously, the earlier in a relationship we make two missions a top priority, the better. And if we can wait to bring children into the equation until when we're both good and ready, better still—and certainly easier.

Make no mistake: it's definitely possible to embark upon the life-work path after kids are present, though it always demands highly creative problem-solving. But before mates can put their heads together, they must first put their hearts together. If they're not dreaming as one, they need to untie, strand by strand, their tangled skein of unresolved conflict and unrestored trust. As they work together to build emotional integrity, they will gain the power to identify and communicate needs and to negotiate to have those needs met. In that emotional safe zone, they will be able to explore their missions in life.

Where there are two wills, hearts joined in love, and lots of support, there's always a way. While in our parents' and grandparents' days, this eighth Natural Law of Love may have appeared extraterrestrial, its time has now come. A healthy unwillingness to overlook talents, miss opportunities, and dissipate love in uncreative busywork is rising like a groundswell under the feet of partners everywhere. Clearly, we're ready to commit to real work that not only inspires, but also makes a difference—improving both home and world. As for home, the impact of two missions per family on the institution of marriage promises to be as awesome as that of state-of-the-art parenting on the next generations of children. As for the world, it will be transformed. As religious leader and philosopher Matthew Fox says, the real crisis in our day is one of work, especially what we're willing to do for money—and the effect our decisions have on our environment, our social systems, our economy, and our children. When we partners support each other in doing what serves each of us best—and therefore helps everyone else—our world will be well on its way to a better future.

Discovering and fleshing out the dual missions within your couple will be a lifelong journey. It's never too early—or too late—to discover your mission in life, whether individually or jointly. And if mission falls dormant in either or both of you at any point in your shared life, you can commit to bring it to blossom again—together! And, if this law presents any roadblocks that Dream Sessions and the follow-up activity that they inspire can't budge, perhaps the additional mission-in-life resources featured in Chapter 10, "Help," will provide the needed muscle.

THE KEY TO MISSION IN LIFE

Committing to discovering and fulfilling your purpose in life is the key to the eighth Natural Law of Love.

This means ...

> 𝕊 Doing work that you're passionate about and that contributes to the greater good.

> 𝕊 Supporting your partner in efforts to do the same.

WALKING

WILLINGNESS AND ABILITY

AS A STATE OF MIND

Some of us know by now that to stay with someone until death parts us is potentially hazardous to our health.

That the undying devotion celebrated in Top Forty songs, romance novels, and television soaps is the stuff of fantasy; that the super-responsible hero husband who rescues the sweet but dependent wife is a tired traditional myth; and that, on a more pragmatic note, to commit to our beloved in such a way that we openendedly relinquish financial responsibility for our own person is a recipe for ruin. We're only too aware that in this crazy world, *anything* can happen—and each one of us needs to be able to generate our own decent income.

Certainly, when we fall in love, we're in a state of intoxication, pure and simple, and our good judgment, even our basic notions of self-care, may temporarily go down the drain. Inarguably, such spells of lovesickness—of thinking he's our knight, she's our baby—are wonderful, sometimes even divine. And the long era when guys paid all the bills had its practical, sensible place in history. The Law of Walking accepts all that as a given. What it's concerned with is exposing the age-old elephants in the living room—the unhealthy emotional and financial dependencies that allow lower-order, survival-based needs to run our relationships. The ninth Natural Law of Love—*the willingness and ability to walk, should it cease to be self-loving for us to remain*—is designed to prevent such dependencies, to keep us from maintaining a relationship for all the wrong reasons, and to promote healthy interdependence. Our litmus test for this interdependence is whether or not we're able to create and stand by the core agreements discussed in Chapter 6.

Remember that all people have both higher-order needs (for self-love, emotional intimacy, and mission in life) and lower-order needs. This latter category has two subsets: physical needs (for food, shelter, and bodily safety) and emotional needs (for a sense of belonging to both parents and tribe). Over the years, the lower-order needs spawned couple traditions that in our era are no longer either beneficial or pragmatic. Even many of us whose lower-order needs have all been met haven't completely rid ourselves of the psychological sense that they're still unfulfilled.

Regardless of the material splendor that might surround us, emotionally we're bumped back into survival mode every time transference comes up with anyone. The real villain, as always, is low self-love. It convinces us that (1) we're incapable of taking care of ourselves materially and will end up destitute if we try, (2) we'll be abandoned or rejected if we assert our true selves, or (3) we'll be punished with some awful combination of both. As these fears crystallize into unconscious blocks and self-fulfilling prophecies, we partners end up either living out our worst nightmare, or (more commonly) living in paralytic fear that our prophecies will come about.

If lack of self-love weren't at issue, we'd be in touch with our natural genius and lovability from the start; we'd have no problem figuring out how to adequately provide for ourselves—materially and emotionally. But it is at issue; and because of it, our lower-order needs have devolved in our romantic relationships into now-obsolete emotional and economic dependencies that activate patterns of self-destructiveness in both women and men. Given the power of those dependencies to ruin lives and love, the ninth Natural Law of Love draws a line in the sand: *we can't really say yes until we're able to say no.*

Walking: A Position of the Heart

This doesn't mean that the ninth Natural Law of Love prescribes separation or divorce. Paradoxical as it may seem, the Law of Walking functions more as a safeguard for the healthy longevity of a relationship than as a license to leave it. For leaving and *being willing and able to leave* are as different as passion fruit and oysters. Willingness and ability to walk comprise a state of mind, a position of the heart—and the ultimate act of self-love. While we never use this law to threaten, manipulate, or punish our beloved, meaning it is its power. Like the martial artist who's never been in a fight, if we're ready to act in defense of our healthy needs, most likely we'll never need to.

The ninth Natural Law of Love asks us to commit to developing our self-love to the point where we're able, from time to time, to honestly reassess our relationship. This means being able to comfortably ask ourselves, "Is this relationship still good for me?"—"Do its challenges contribute to my self-actualization, or do they inhibit me?"—"Am I inspired to grow and is my sense of self expanding, or do I feel compromised and limited?"—"Does this relationship support who I really am and who I want to become?"

What Walking Isn't: The Nonsolution of Leaving

Certainly, as we all know only too well, leaving is an already overused solution, with one in two American marriages ending in divorce. But we can't stress it enough: *we're not talking about leaving.* We're talking about the *willingness and ability* to leave. The fact is a good number of us in that fifty-percent-divorce camp don't walk out of our relationships anyway—we run. And most of us give up without getting good help. In other words, we're not coming from a position of *willingness and ability*.

Bolting is frequently the result of not having been willing and able to take care of ourselves from the very beginning. We may, for example, have failed to set boundaries or define and communicate our needs—sometimes even the most basic needs, such as our need for sexual exclusivity or our need not to be put down.

Indeed, we may have lacked the requisite self-love to be able to create any conditions for relationship whatsoever (even in our imagination), let alone core agreements. Without those boundaries and conditions to communicate and defend our self-respecting bottom line, our only defense alternative when we're under siege is to pull out the big guns. But "I don't love you anymore" is an awful way to tell our mate that our needs aren't being met.

In some ways, divorce might seem to be the modern solution to our marital problems—an affirmation that we can stand alone and don't need to rely on the couple—but of course it's not. Even those of us who ultimately bolt don't usually arrive at the decision quickly or easily. The process itself is excruciating; in fact, it can bring up more fear and grief than the prospect of death itself. What's more, as everyone knows, broken marriages create chaos for our whole society, not to mention for our kids. No, divorce isn't a *solution*. It's simply the only recourse most of us are aware of when we don't know how to figure out, and then directly communicate, what we really need in order to stay in trust and in love with another person—especially when material or psychological dependencies get in the way.

Here's the irony, though: very often the partner who leaves a marriage is fed up with behavior that he or she tolerated out of fear that the other partner would run off. In such a couple it's dependence, not love, that holds the union together. And unless the underlying dependence needs are addressed, they'll taint the next relationship as well—and the next and the next. Some second-timers, lacking insight as to why their first marriage foundered, plunge into an identical mess; others take a reactionary swing, bonding with what they hope is an opposite type of person. In addition to outrageous divorce rates, we have equally discouraging success rates on second marriages.

This is not to say that divorce is never appropriate. As every good physician can confirm, sometimes it's necessary to amputate. But divorce is tragic when, with foresight, it could have been avoided—in other words, when it's the result of failing, at the beginning of our relationship, to examine potential areas of emotional or financial dependence (areas that might inhibit us from knowing our needs and seeking to have them met) and then set basic conditions for our relationship.

What Walking Isn't: The Nonsolution of Staying

We hate the pain of divorce. Still, longevity in and of itself *is not a virtue.* It's equally tragic when we stay with someone despite severe dysfunction—until our relationship kills us or death really does break us apart. That sort of hanging on by the fingernails poisons our whole family and can do a worse number on the kids than divorce itself. Like those who separate due to unaddressed dependencies, we hangers-on also often refuse to avail ourselves of even the gentlest outside help. Our problem is that, seized by survival fears from the get-go, we're unwilling and unable to leave. No one taught us the age-old wisdom that the best way to hold onto something is to be willing and able to let it go; that when we face the fears involved in surrendering something dear to us—even the love of our life—those fears don't have to turn into self-fulfilling prophecies.

Dependencies: When We Won't Rock the Boat

Whether it's our style to cut and run or to insist that what has no life breathes still, the underlying problem is always the same: our fear of rocking the boat. And yet the only reason a few waves are so scary is that we're dependent on our partner, whether emotion-

171

ally, financially, or both. Often we just feel safer leaving things somewhat vague, for when we honestly communicate our terms, our core conditions, we expose the parameters of our relationship. *This alone can seem to threaten its existence.*

So what could make our financial or emotional dependencies so strong that we're afraid to express what we need? The cause, as you may have guessed, is unhealed childhood trauma. And as we said in Chapter 3, emotional trauma bumps us down into our lower-order needs. In the case of emotional dependencies, we might be terrified that we'll be abandoned by our mate (our symbolic parent, thanks to transference) or that a failed marriage will cause us to be rejected by other people—namely, our tribe. If our problem is material dependence, the terror is that we won't have what we need to make it as physical beings. Either way, on some level it feels as if *we can't survive without this other person.* Dependent on the relationship, we're therefore desperate for it not to end; so we withhold from each other precisely the information we both need in order to nourish our chemistry and keep our relationship healthy and well.

But Don't We Know Better?

Like all the previous trauma discussions in this book, these revelations seem to fly in the face of our contemporary image of ourselves. And it's true: most of us are generally pretty savvy on the subject of personal power and autonomy, both monetary and psychological. The feminist revolution dramatically brought home to us the disastrous impact, especially on women, of delegating responsibility for our material well-being to another, and the recovery movement indelibly named not only chemical addictions for us, but also the "people addiction" of codependence (the kind of emotional dependence in which we're preoccupied with another as a way to avoid ourselves).

Sometimes seen as a women's problem, codependence is actually gender-neutral. Male codependence can play out at work, where men often unconsciously strive to win the approval of male colleagues and superiors—stand-ins for their dads—or at home, where they sometimes take "too much care" of their girlfriends and wives. On the home front, codependent men exhibit not only the standard codependent placating behavior, but also the far more complex (and perhaps more typically male) "allergy to intimacy" that shows up as shutting down, distancing, or bolting. Men develop these maneuvers as little boys as a response to being emotionally "smothered" or made to caretake a parent, usually a mother, in obvious or subtle ways. What most of us don't realize is that these parental triggers are actually forms of abandonment: parents who smother or demand caretaking are needy, not nourishing; they're not "there" emotionally for their kids.

Boys who live with that sort of abandonment grow into men who keep thick walls around themselves or withdraw reflexively when confronted with even healthy emotional expression. They've got quick reflexes around any behavior in a partner that remotely resembles neediness. And yet they're needy themselves: like all of us suffering from early abandonment, these cool guys are emotionally dependent. But try to convince a codependent man of that and he'll say, "Who me, emotionally dependent? How can I be dependent when I need my space so badly that it's a constant source of static between my wife and me?"

All healthy adults routinely need time alone, yet if we were emotionally suffocated by our caregivers as children, we can't help but transfer the problem onto our mate—which makes our need for breathing room feel gargantuan. While we'll eventually have to work through the transference and the underlying trauma, we still need our space, and we must honor that need rather than keeping it hidden so as not to rock the boat.

Many "distancers" protest that they didn't realize time to themselves would be such an intense need until they were well into the relationship, or that they'd never been taught to negotiate. Alternatively, their justification might be that they had brought it

up, but their girlfriend had been so hurt (or angry) with this perceived rejection that pushing for solitude simply wasn't worth it.
Distancers can't tolerate reactions of hurt or anger in others,
because their young selves feel threatened that they'll lead their
partner to leave them. If not for that fear, such men (and more and
more women in this category) would stay the course and simply
insist that their partner negotiate so that privacy needs get met.

This terribly common couple dilemma veils distancers' dependence on their partners. It not only falsely stereotypes them as more
independent, but also scapegoats their mates—traditionally
women—as the only emotionally dependent ones. The reality,
however, is that both suffer from emotional dependencies; in fact,
as we noted earlier, they're dependent *to precisely the same degree.*

Like emotional dependence, material dependence is a response
to danger. The only difference is that now the child part of us feels
threatened about its physical well-being; in other words, the lower-
order survival needs for eating, being sheltered, or staying safe are
kicking in. Again, early trauma is to blame—in this case, survival
trauma. Whether that trauma was literal (such as losing our house
through repossession or fire) or abstract (such as perceiving and
absorbing our parents' Depression-era anxieties), it has powerful
long-term effects on our ability to create or stand by self-loving
conditions for relationship.

Thanks to gender conditioning, one of the ways men typically
deal with their survival fears is by becoming frenetic wage-earners.
Some women also choose that "male" route, becoming super-
achievers and creating security for themselves. More typically,
though, women fall deeper under the spell of the trance of tradition, becoming financial dependents. Thirty years into the
women's movement, the monkey is still on our back: the fact of
"women who earn too little" is still an ongoing crisis. Indeed,
every day countless women enter romantic unions in a relative
financial fog, while others, often with dependent children, find
themselves penniless due to divorce or desertion.

While some of us struggle more with material dependence than others, none of us escaped as children the early scenarios that lead adults to feel inadequate, uncherished, or bereft of resources—and subsequently dependent in various ways. Understanding the roots of this kind of human frailty helps partners develop compassion about dependencies, whether our own or each other's. If, for example, our partner was shamed while learning to read, she might end up disliking school, avoiding higher education, and concluding that she could never support herself; and then she might unconsciously react by seeking out a wealthy man to lean on. Or if our mate was esteemed by his parents only when he performed well in school and sports, he might fear that he couldn't attract a woman except as provider.

When partners feel safe enough to tell each other about these bits of their individual histories, a new empathy emerges for their current predicaments, which they now understand as symptoms of their pasts. Whatever the source of our partners' dependencies, we must never mislabel them as weakness. Instead, they must be known for what they are: unhealed childhood dents in our self-confidence that end up as craters in our self-love.

Damaged Discernment

The first step toward developing compassion for ourselves about our dependencies is recognizing those dependencies—not an easy task. It takes a tremendous amount of self-love and, yes, guts to face the fact that we're dependent on a relationship that's hurting us. Denial, rationalization, and minimization are emotional dependence's favorite disguises. They raise our threshold for pain and numb us to the unacceptability of our situation. The more intense our abandonment trauma, the stickier these psychic glues, and the more confused we'll be. Because emotional dependence damages our discernment, we end up unable to determine what we want or need and thus are incapable of recognizing when we should say no, insist on fairness, get help, or walk.

Extreme circumstances have an advantage, odd as that may seem. When our relationships are glaringly unhealthy, the pain more quickly becomes undeniable. Substance abuse, infidelity, and violence leave little room for positive interpretation. That's why the Law of Peacemaking presents these transgressions as the center of the New Couple's core agreements. Unfortunately, though, the most destructive emotional dependencies are subtle. Problems are usually quietly and systematically denied—often for an astonishingly long time.

Transcending Depending

All this knowledge about the universality of dependencies notwithstanding, *insight isn't healing* (as Sigmund Freud first observed), though we wish it were. Beneath all our dependencies hides that mildly to severely traumatized inner child, quaking in fear that we'll fail, that everything will be taken away, or that we'll be abandoned. Until the trauma is healed for that inner child, our dependencies will continue to bruise us. But as we saw in earlier chapters, the healing of early trauma takes not only emotional integrity and the willingness to work through transferences; it also demands time and a heartfelt commitment from both of us.

Say we make that commitment to deal with our dependencies and embark on the road to true interdependence, undertaking to heal our emotional and survival fears. How exactly do we proceed? Well, while nothing will happen overnight, this book has everything partners need to make a powerful start. The good news is that when as a couple we embrace the other nine Natural Laws of Love, our healing begins, and we're automatically on our way to healthy autonomy.

Picking a partner based on chemistry keeps us from focusing on attributes, such as wealth and status, that could foster dependencies. Priority helps us identify the behaviors that allow us to avoid our feelings, while emotional integrity teaches us how to express and manage those feelings. Deep listening keeps the air clear between us and tunes up our trust, while equality averts buildups of injustice, gross and tiny. Peacemaking gives us agreements so that we can get specific about our bottom lines, and self-love first shows us the nature of that which still scares us from the past and then helps us dissolve such hurts. Mission in life makes sure that we do something that matters, which builds our confidence to provide for ourselves in a joyful (but still material) way. And whatever dependencies we can't make healing headway with using these laws, we tackle with "Help."

Traditional Marriage and the Inability to Walk

Many of us watched our parents' marriage wither because our traditional mother and father wouldn't or couldn't stand by what they wanted in life or love. Others of us grew up in homes that were broken because these same needs were expressed only when it was far too late.

In the early days, willingness and ability to walk—and the emotional and financial autonomy which that combination represents—would have been antithetical to the purpose of marriage itself, which was largely to institutionalize the meeting of lower-order needs. Thus our forebears committed to a union for life. Though rigid, this arrangement enjoyed its place in the evolution of male-female relationships and obviously achieved its ends.

Later, at least in Western society, men and women started to marry for love. These latter-day traditionals were free to choose from their hearts. It could be said that the romantic traditional couple was granted a new freedom: to fall both in—and out—of love. And if precious love ever got lost, the partners didn't "have to" stay. Unfortunately, that didn't mean they were willing and able to walk *while they were together*. Those who stayed rarely recognized their own needs, set boundaries and conditions (at least in their minds) for continuing to stay, or took self-loving action were these boundaries transgressed. Though romantic traditionals married for love, the early institution of marriage still locked them into roles related to survival.

Furthermore, even those needs that were acknowledged weren't translated into agreements. Beyond the big agreement—that couples stay together for life—there was no structure to protect a wide spectrum of individual values and goals, from monogamy and nonviolence to the pursuit of individual dreams.

As the survival imperative softened, women started working outside the home, alimony allowed a financial freedom of sorts, and divorce came into vogue. However, though the traditional shackles of marriage had been loosened, couples were often loathe to break up (even when divorce might have been the healthiest option) because to do so would violate the integrity of the family. "Staying together for the kids" justified the preservation of countless embattled and lifeless marriages. An unquestioned societal and religious norm, the child-rationalized union often had the power to preclude either partner from being willing or able to walk— from being able, sometimes, even to think about it—regardless of the circumstances. Violence, incest, and substance addictions, and the devastating impact of such abuses, weren't good-enough excuses to walk even for those same kids.

Clearly, the idea that staying together for the kids serves their emotional needs can be a grave miscalculation (even when well intentioned). But many traditional parents, like many parents today, simply couldn't conceive that *kids suffer far more in unhappily married homes than in conscientiously separated homes.* Other parents used protection of the kids as a rationalization for perpetuating a withered union. Marriages preserved for children masked not only brassbound adherence to traditional family and gender norms, but also (more to the point of our discussion of walking) deep-seated personal dependencies, whether economic, emotional, or both.

Because men generally earned the main income in traditional homes, they did have a certain edge—they were in possession of their own economic resources. Therefore, if their marriage was on the rocks, they (unlike their economically dependent wives) were ostensibly free to walk. And unquestionably, some did jump ship. Those who did so legally and through all the proper channels "paid through the nose" in alimony and child support. The deserters, on the other hand, taking advantage of the lax laws of the day, left dependent wives and children to fend for themselves. The fact remains that neither the irresponsible ones, nor those who ended up writing checks to their exes for decades, were willing and able to walk when it counted—from the start of the relationship.

How about the men who hung in there—those whose chemistry was killed in the power struggle but stayed in the marriage nevertheless, playing the dutiful husband? More obviously unwilling or unable to walk, these partners were victims of the mythological roles of male-provider and family-leader. In addition to their fears of the opinions of the outside world—fears, for example, of being seen as failing as a family man, being branded irresponsible, or otherwise being cast out from the tribe—these traditional breadwinners had to contend with their own often ruthless "inner sexists": they judged themselves by the balance of their bank account and their ability to provide security. Their need to be needed was as desperate as the clamoring of the so-called needy ones at home.

Traditional wives, on the other hand, were economic dependents; they didn't "work." In their cherished roles as homemakers, they made their husbands and children their mission. Although these women enjoyed certain economic benefits, this work was unsalaried and, for the most part, uninsured. In other words, if they lost their "job"—through divorce or their spouse's death—their income stood to take a nosedive. Given that financial constraint, traditional wives risked a dramatic decline in material well-being if they walked. But economic dependencies weren't the only thing that trapped these wives in marriage. Willingness was a rare commodity too. Even the wealthiest fell victim to the standard rash of emotional dependencies: fear of abandonment, fear of being alone, fear of who they'd be if stripped of the mythic good-wife-and-mother status—all these weighed heavily upon them.

At the outer limits was the ultimate inability to walk: "learned helplessness." This severe form of emotional dependence robs us of our capacity to take action on our own behalf, even in the face of danger. Because it's revealed progressively in adult relationships, the helplessness does appear to be learned; the fact is, however, this terrible emotional ill is the result of traumatic abandonment in childhood—abandonment that's later retriggered. Learned helplessness explains why wives allow themselves to be disrespect-ed, degraded, even battered. Though the traditional wife didn't have the benefit of this psychological classification—and, in addi-tion to the brutality at home, was frequently judged by the out-side world to be morally weak—the learned helplessness syndrome is still very much with us today.

In fact, today a mild form is often found in traditional wives who start out with careers. Although financially able to walk, these women are emotionally unwilling—if not unable—to do so once they're parents. The symbolic creation of a "new family" evokes the inner child, replete with her inability for self-care, and sudden-ly personal needs are subjugated to those of the husband and fam-ily. In that process, formerly independent traditionals lose their autonomy and identity at home; and sometimes they lose confi-dence in their ability to make a living as well.

Striving for Interdependence

The ideal couple state is true interdependence. In that state, each of us is a financially viable, emotionally autonomous entity, and that grounding allows us to enjoy true emotional intimacy with our beloved. When as individuals we have both the internal stance of being willing to walk and the external stance of being able to walk—in other words, when we have enough and are

enough unto ourselves—we're free to be as supportive and generous as our hearts desire, without fear of being drained of our energy, goodwill, or resources. As though by alchemical reaction, our
peak-performance New Couple state produces an environment of
abundance in which both of us can relax and thrive.

That's a beautiful ideal for us all to strive for. Meantime, as
we've said, down here on earth we're all wrestling with tiresome
dependencies and various and sundry areas of low self-love. As
with power imbalances and unfairness, just acknowledging our
dependencies is half the battle won. Still, it's only reasonable to
expect our life together to present us with times during which we
absolutely have to depend on each other. As part of our search for
mission in life, for example, we might ask our partner to support
us while we go back to school. And when we're challenged by circumstances—the loss of a job, the death of a parent, the birth of
a child—we depend on our partner emotionally, often feeling that
we couldn't scrape by without our beloved other. Although super-
ficially these periods might mimic lapses into dependence, they
are, in fact, the essence of interdependence. As such, they prove
precious in crystallizing everlasting bonds of the heart.

What the ninth Natural Law of Love asks of us is that, at the
end of the day, we alternate between dependence and supportive-
ness as circumstances dictate, that we work toward the realization
of emotional and economic symmetry, and that we trust each
other's commitment to the ideal of interdependence. This heady
stuff of the new exchange sounds good, but wishing won't make it
so. Interdependence requires all the Natural Laws of Love. The
sixth, the Law of Peacemaking, with its powerful agreements,
often gets an especially good workout. It takes good intentions
and lots of practice to set healthy, self-loving limits without judging, manipulating, or otherwise trying to coerce our partner.

The interdependence that the Law of Walking fosters has differing advantages for both genders. For a woman, the "freedom to
stay"—to remain in the union because she wants to, not because

she needs to—gives her a bottom line, which builds the healthy self-reliance she so yearns for. Never again will she have to feel trapped in an unhappy marriage. On her way to freedom, she'll find herself empowered and able to develop the so-called masculine attributes of initiative, goal-setting, and assertiveness (if she doesn't already have them). She'll be proud of herself in a way her mother most likely never was.

For a man, the "freedom to stay" only if he wants to releases him from the tyranny of his assumed role as economic provider. Formerly dominated by responsibility, he now can say no: never again will he have to linger duty-bound and guilt-tripped in a loveless union. His need to be needed, which concealed a shadow dependence on women, now can heal, because he knows that his partner can survive without him but chooses to stay with him out of love. In a truly interdependent partnership, he can safely exercise his new emotional honesty and be supported in developing the so-called feminine attributes of trust, openness, nurturance, and receptivity.

Men and women alike will find that a commitment to the Law of Walking allows self-love to soar and frees both partners to know their own power and live their dreams. This law asks that we measure the parameters of our dependencies and explore their potential bases—be they fear of loneliness or rejection, fear of not being able to protect ourselves or cope on our own, fear of growing old alone, fear of having no value unless we're part of a couple, or fear that we can't support ourselves materially. By committing to this law we tell our partner that our self-love is so solid that we won't accept the unacceptable, we cement our own intention to stand by our needs via the agreements we create, and we learn how to really trust ourselves and our favorite other. *Love will not be lost in the process.*

THE KEY TO WALKING

Striving for interdependence and individual autonomy in your couple—that is, being willing and able
to walk in order to stay together in healthy union—
is the key to the Ninth Natural Law of Love.
This means exploring and committing to resolve:

❖ Financial dependencies
❖ Emotional dependencies

CATALYZE THE GROWTH PROCESS

Help is the ultimate Natural Law of Love. Our commitment to it as a couple means that we each agree to call a snag a snag, however large it may loom. It's our pledge that we'll go right to the cutting edge and take full advantage of the most sophisticated, heartfelt, and amazing educational and healing opportunities that exist.

What's more, we'll keep trying new opportunities until we've broken through. Our commitment to the Law of Help represents our promise to stop at nothing to make our relationship as successful as it can possibly be.

In terms of all the Natural Laws of Love, the tenth could provide no grander finale. It functions as a jump-start at those times when we find ourselves stalled on any of the earlier nine laws. And almost every couple will stall somewhere, sometime. Even those of us who are able to embrace all the laws intellectually occasionally encounter obstacles applying some or all of them. Commitment to the Law of Help means that whenever that happens, we'll do something about it—namely, get our self—or ourselves—to an expert. Unlike the Law of Chemistry, over which we really have no power—we either have it with each other, or we don't—this final law points up all the ways we do have power over laws two through nine. It's about everything we can learn and heal, and thus it offers the surest hope for the actual fulfillment of our higher-order needs.

Help is different from the regular, didactic kind of education, in that it both instructs the head and moves the heart. It helps us not only grasp concepts, gain insights, and acquire skills, but also heal on a deep emotional level (and hence grow and mature). Some types of Help can even offer a quantum leap in self-love, which is something every partner craves. Indeed, since such education has the potential to renew—even recreate—us as partners and as persons, it is nothing less than transformational.

Our hope is that this book is itself an agent of Help—that a close reading will not only teach but also catalyze a growth process in you and your relationship. The other forms of this special kind of education introduced in this chapter are counseling and psychotherapy (couple, individual, and group); support groups, including Twelve-Step recovery programs; and workshops, intensives, and retreats. Websites and phone numbers for various educational options are cited at the end of this chapter.

It's not easy to ask for relationship help, in part because "shrinks" and "getting shrunk" have been caricatured for decades. Hollywood hasn't helped at all: movies typically portray therapists as pathetic, unappealing, unethical, neurotic, or stark, raving mad. Those adjectives do apply to some therapists (as they do to every category of professional), but there are great therapists out there too—lots of them—and they're worth hunting down. Fortunately, exceptions that do justice to the profession also exist on film. The movies *Ordinary People*, *The Prince of Tides*, and *Good Will Hunting*, for example, present complex and compelling portraits of dedicated (if overly involved) practitioners for whom psychotherapy is a mission in life. And each one succeeds in conveying the life-changing potential and magic of the encounter between therapist and client.

Contemporary films also reflect society's rigid taboo against counseling—the public misconception that there has to be something desperately wrong with us to justify getting help, that help is appropriate only as a frantic last-ditch effort before crisis or breakdown. This is patently untrue: individuals and couples with garden-variety problems are helped every day by counseling. Still, the societal stigma against "talk therapy" is toxically shaming; it would have us believe that "submitting" to an hour in front of a therapeutically trained helper proves that we've failed or are weak, self-indulgent, unresourceful, or "too Californian"—and, perhaps worst of all, at risk for being rejected by our partner or tribe (or both). That's why committing to the Law of Help is as revolutionary as it is profound. Such a commitment demonstrates our absolute dedication, as partners, to keeping our love and trust alive—whatever it takes.

What's Out There and How to Shop

Of the three main categories of Help available to us—counseling and psychotherapy, group work, and workshops—counseling is usually our first recourse when we hit a snag in applying the Natural Laws of Love. (The terms *counseling* and *psychotherapy* have been used interchangeably throughout this book. They're not quite synonymous, however, as the later discussion reveals.)

COUNSELING

Counselors come in many different stripes; their backgrounds vary widely, as do their focuses. *Psychologists* have a Ph.D. (doctorate of philosophy in psychology) or a Psy.D. (doctorate of psychology); *psychiatrists* have an MD (doctorate of medicine with a specialization in psychiatry); *psychotherapists* and *counselors* have an MA or an MS (master of arts or science degree in counseling or clinical psychology); and *clinical social workers* have an MA or an MS (master of arts or science degree in clinical social work).

We recommend that you choose a specialist who possesses at

least a master's degree in counseling, clinical psychology, or clinical social work (or who is an intern in such a master's degree program) and is appropriately licensed. (The licensing issue can be confusing, because states have different licensure requirements and sometimes have different names for practitioners, and most countries outside the USA have no mental health licensure at all.)

While each individual practitioner will define his or her work slightly differently, psychotherapists and psychologists (who often call themselves psychotherapists as well) generally specialize in depth work and are more likely to work with childhood issues. Still, some counselors do this too, and some psychologists and psychotherapists don't.

The first step in identifying a professional from whom to seek help is soliciting recommendations from trusted associates—perhaps the family doctor or lawyer, a clergyperson, a family member, or a friend. Whether an individual or couple therapist, the practitioner selected must feel warm and empathetic and must inspire trust. Chemistry matters here, as it does in intimate relationships, although real rapport will take time to develop. As always, intuition should be relied on.

COUPLE COUNSELING

Couple counseling is typically conducted by a single practitioner working one-on-two with the couple. (Teams of couple co-therapists do exist, however; and for the balance they afford, they offer certain advantages. They can be hard to find, though, and married ones, like the authors, are even more rare.)

Any help sought from a professional must be compatible with the Ten Natural Laws of Love. In order to support these laws, a couple counselor must specialize in working with the transference that exists between partners. Additionally, he or she (or they) needs to be competent in the specific aspect of the law that's posing the problem. A good place to begin the search is with couple counselors trained by relationship expert and author Harville

Hendrix, whose approach complements the one in this book.

It's appropriate to ask a few questions over the phone before booking an appointment. Questions can determine, for example, whether the therapist specializes in working with couple transference. If the answer is yes, additional questions can focus on the specific law and then the particular issue that's causing difficulty. If the practitioner has expertise in this specific area as well (and isn't off-putting over the phone), it's worth booking an initial interview to find out whether there's a "fit" between all three (or four) parties.

Murray Bowen, one of the fathers of so-called family therapy, asserts that practitioners can take clients only as far as they themselves have gone in their own growth and healing. It's true that it can be extremely helpful to work with someone who's "been there," who's actually walking the talk and has been a client in couple counseling. Although it's not professional for therapists to reveal personal details, that issue is worth asking about in general terms. Many excellent therapists prefer to remain as anonymous as possible, however, which is a valid ethical stance. Whether they answer the question or not, their response will likely convey a sense of who they are as people and what sort of fit would result.

Since trust is the foundation of a viable client-therapist relationship, it's imperative that the couple therapist chosen be someone with whom both partners feel gut-level comfort and whom they sense they can eventually trust. Sometimes counseling can edge people out of their "comfort zone." Those "labor pains" shouldn't be mistaken for a poor fit, however. Still, no one should feel obligated to make a counseling relationship work that lacks connection or chemistry; it's the therapist's job to serve clients, not the clients' job to keep him or her from feeling rejected. Therefore, the therapist chosen must meet all of the above criteria.

INDIVIDUAL COUNSELING AND COACHING

For some partners in distress, application of these laws might involve individual counseling as either an adjunct to couple work or on its own. In order to be compatible with the Ten Natural Laws of Love, individual counseling (like couple counseling) must combine intellectual insight with emotional process work. Additionally, the therapist's clinical orientation must focus on individuation from family-of-origin or inner-child work; recovery from codependence, toxic guilt, and toxic shame; transference between therapist and client; and recovery from childhood emotional trauma, including all forms of abuse and neglect. Such a practitioner will typically identify their orientation as "psychodynamic."

Specializations appropriate to the laws include EMDR (eye movement desensitization reprocessing, a gentle but highly effective psychotherapeutic technique for resolving emotional trauma), breathwork (including holotropic breathing and rebirthing), primal therapy, Gestalt therapy, psychosynthesis, and somatic, or body-oriented, psychotherapy. Although they are not required for getting unstuck on any of the Natural Laws of Love, all of these are excellent modalities for augmenting emotional awareness and release. Because the power and intensity of the above techniques shouldn't be underestimated, they're recommended only in the hands of practitioners who are trained psychotherapists (though some truly gifted healers provide exception).

The healer-heal-thyself maxim is as applicable to individual counselors as it is to those who work with couples, as is the need for chemistry and trust. Therefore, the earlier guidelines for selecting an acceptable couple specialist are all relevant, including the step of asking the practitioner if he or she has undergone counseling. As before, questions focused on issues of concern can help determine whether client and prospective practitioner are on the same page.

Individual consultation that addresses career or vocational aspirations is also compatible with several of the Natural Laws of Love. The career-vocational guidance field has changed significantly in recent years. A new crop of vocational counselors—now usually called *life coaches* or just *coaches* (but sometimes also *personal, career, job,* or *dream coaches*)—have raised this kind of counseling to the level of art. Instead of looking just for what people do well—or trying to corral them into areas where jobs are available—they assess the seven areas of intelligence and make use of discussion, visualization, and intuition rather than standardized aptitude tests. These coaches need not meet the professional criteria for psychotherapists, but it's important that they feel warm, empathetic, and responsible, that they inspire trust, and that they come highly recommended.

GROUP WORK

The second type of Help that can be applied in conjunction with a commitment to the Natural Laws of Love is group work. The two principal types of groups are therapy groups and support groups. While the former are generally facilitated by trained professionals, both are capable of delivering a profoundly healing experience.

THERAPY GROUPS

Many kinds of therapy groups exist, offering potent healing and growth experiences. Some of these groups are for couples, though these tend to spring up erratically and can be hard to locate. The same criteria outlined above for choosing a couple therapist (including experience with transference work) apply to therapy groups. In order to ensure complete emotional safety, it's essential that these groups be led by a credentialed therapist with special training in running groups.

Group therapy for individuals can also be highly therapeutic, especially when it's topic-focused, addressing such issues as eating disorders, childhood abuse, anger management, and incest. Bereavement or grief groups are extremely helpful following the death of a loved one. The criteria for groups would match those stated above for individual therapy.

Another group option is a program of co-counseling known as Co-Counseling and Re-evaluation Counseling. Actually a short class, this low-cost, grassroots alternative to psychotherapy has a large international following. It trains participants in emotional-release work (catharsis) so that after completing several months of classes, they can pair up with other graduates and counsel each other free of charge. The techniques are simple, powerful, and revolutionary, as are the many books by its originator, Harvey Jackins.

SUPPORT GROUPS

Designed to provide emotional support on an ever-growing variety of issues, support groups are typically—though not always—leaderless and either low-fee or free of charge. Most popular are the Twelve-Step programs for recovery from any number of addictions or compulsive behaviors: Alcoholics Anonymous (AA), Narcotics Anonymous (NA), Workaholics Anonymous (WA), Sex and Love Addicts Anonymous (SLAA), Overeaters Anonymous (OA), Debtors Anonymous (DA), and Gamblers Anonymous (GA).

Other Twelve-Step groups provide support for codependents (CODA), family members of alcoholics (Al-Anon), family members of drug addicts (Nar-Anon), adult children of alcoholics (ACA/ACOA), adult children of mentally ill parents (ACMIP), incest survivors (SIA), and those with other special issues. (Many of the groups listed above offer women-only, men-only, gay, lesbian, and/or bisexual orientations as well.) "Men's" and "women's" groups, groups for singles or divorcé(e)s, and groups focusing on issues such as emotional support, life-mission or life-purpose identification, life-transition work, accountability, or fertility exist in abundance and can benefit a couple in applying specific laws.

WORKSHOPS, INTENSIVES, SPECIAL COURSES, AND RETREATS

The category of workshops, intensives, special courses, and retreats, though underutilized, often offers the best results of all the modern varieties of Help. Some, though not all, of these options are pricey; nevertheless, because they promise (and generally deliver) a substantial amount of growth and healing—even remarkable breakthroughs—in a short period of time, they end up being cost-effective.

Though the majority of workshops are designed for individuals, couple-oriented options do exist. These include NewCouple seminars, Harville Hendrix's Getting All the Love You Want couple workshops, Marriage Encounter and Engagement Encounter workshops, and couple retreats, intimacy weekends, and relationship trainings produced by other organizations. The best referral sources are relationship experts, therapists, churches, and word of mouth.

Among the intensives and workshops designed for individuals, those most compatible with the Ten Natural Laws of Love are those that focus on the inner child, relationships with parents, and healing the emotions. All are most effective when attended as an adjunct to individual or couple therapy. Among the vast number of options, the quality can vary from superb to questionable. Therefore, the recommendation of professionals or trusted friends is essential.

Both the weeklong Hoffman Quadrinity Process and the ten-day Star Process have excellent international reputations. For many participants, they're equivalent to months of psychotherapy and result in a quantum leap in self-love. Participants should only attend under the supervision of an individual or couple counselor, preferably one familiar with the programs. Trainings that facilitate participants in becoming their most authentic self (such as Lee Glickstein's Speaking Circles) can also be highly compatible with the aims of this book, as can life-purpose, assertiveness, financial-empowerment, and personal-empowerment courses (such as Impact Bay Area, which integrates self-defense).

HELP: LAW BY LAW

In this section, we'll look at each of the Ten Natural Laws of Love, identifying issues on which couples typically get stuck and highlighting styles of Help that are especially suitable for each. (The listing is intended to be suggestive rather than exhaustive.)

Chemistry

The waning of our best-friendship or sexual chemistry (or both) are serious problems. If we've experienced New Couple chemistry at some point in our relationship, a decline is always a symptom pointing somewhere in the nine other laws. The first step in addressing a chemistry problem is to review the laws and determine which are out of balance.

If we've never experienced sexual chemistry with anyone—including a partner to whom we're highly attracted and with whom we enjoy best-friendship chemistry—we might be experiencing a symptom of some kind of unresolved issue in our history. Individual psychotherapy may be appropriate. When addressing sexual issues, the gender of the therapist is extremely important.

Priority

The main reason we're unable to prioritize an intimate relationship is codependence with people outside our couple—usually members of the family-of-origin or close friends. Codependence with family members is actually a crisis of psychological individuation, the inability to stand among adults as a peer.

Many forms of Help help us heal codependence and resolve individuation issues. The Twelve-Step group called Codependents Anonymous (CODA) is the treatment of choice for codependence. It's most powerful when attended in tandem with individual psychotherapy with a codependence expert. Though we're often not aware of it, early emotional abandonment can underlie both codependence and our inability to individuate. Assertiveness

193

training—and other self-empowerment courses, such as Impact Self-Defense—and men's and women's groups and co-counseling are all highly indicated in the recovery of codependence. Finally, the workshops, intensives, special courses, and retreats listed above are also excellent.

Help is also appropriate for the kind of codependence that occurs within couples. This codependence can be seen when we're overly preoccupied with our partner and the attention is nonreciprocal, or when we're in a relationship with a mate who's verbally, psychologically, or physically abusive or who suffers from an addiction, compulsion, or mental illness but declines treatment. In both instances, the relationship can't be mutually prioritized. This type of codependence can be addressed using the same kinds of help listed above for codependence with persons outside the couple.

Substance addictions and compulsive behaviors—including the eating disorders of anorexia nervosa, bulimia, and compulsive overeating, as well as alcoholism, drug addiction, workaholism, and gambling—also keep us from being able to prioritize our couple, and they always need outside help. In extreme cases, hospitalization or a period in a rehabilitation center is necessary. Anonymous groups exist for almost every conceivable process and substance addiction, and they continue to be the most effective treatment for maintaining sobriety.

Whereas individual and couple therapy can often be effective at recognizing an addiction or compulsion, we can't expect such therapy to resolve any other problem until the addiction (including codependence) is being addressed and treated. Nor, of course, can we work effectively on any of the Ten Natural Laws of Love if an addictive problem ails us and we're not in recovery for it.

Emotional Integrity

The most common challenges associated with the third Natural Law of Love include emotional illiteracy, which is the inability to get in touch with our feelings and articulate them using I-statements; emotional dishonesty, which is the inability to acknowledge our true feelings to our mate, as well as any buttons, blind spots, and issues that affect either partner; and emotional mismanagement, which is the inability to express negative feelings responsibly. All three categories of Help positively affect our ability to take responsibility for our emotions. Especially effective are individual and couple counseling, co-counseling, breathwork, and special courses such as the Hoffman Process and the Star Process. For help with emotional awareness in particular, breathwork, primal therapy, and Gestalt therapy can all facilitate breakthroughs.

For issues related to emotional trauma—evidenced in our buttons, blind spots, phobias, excessive anxiety or panic, sexual jealousy, rage, and "neurotic" or "control freak" behaviors—individual psychotherapy with a psychodynamically-oriented therapist trained in EMDR or somatics is a good first recourse. Unresolved grief from death of a loved one can be best dealt with in a grief or bereavement group (often offered through churches, hospitals, or hospices) and individual psychotherapy with a grief specialist. Grief over other major losses, including the death of a pet or the loss of material goods due to crime or disaster, can be managed in individual psychotherapy or specialized group therapy. Because major life trauma, such as the death of a child or the inability to conceive, is a major cause of divorce and emotional estrangement between partners, expert individual psychotherapy can be critical to the relationship.

Deep Listening

If we're unable to develop the skill of generally listening from the heart or listening well in Sessions, we can make great inroads in individual counseling and couple counseling. Speaking Circles also specialize in teaching individuals how to deeply listen; thus attendance at intensives or participation in ongoing groups with this focus can produce breakthroughs. Additionally, men's, women's, and emotional support groups that provide excellent opportunities to both deeply listen and be deeply listened to without comment or interruption can help bring this skill into our couple.

Equality

If we find ourselves in a relationship characterized by entrenched gender-based inequalities, couple and individual counseling can help balance things out, as can group therapy for couples and gender-specific support groups. Mates who are on the lower end of the power differential (and dissatisfied with this status) might also benefit from Codependents Anonymous, co-counseling, personal-empowerment courses, assertiveness training, and emotional healing intensives such as the Hoffman Process and the Star Process.

Peacemaking

For anger management and/or conflict resolution, tremendous help is available. If we're unable to initiate a time-out, couple counseling and individual psychotherapy with a focus on codependence, general trauma, or abandonment trauma would be a good starting point. Codependents Anonymous, co-counseling, personal-empowerment courses, assertiveness training, and emotional healing intensives are all recommended as well.

If we're unable to honor a time-out or use the Path to Peace due to out-of-control anger, or if we recognize that we're sitting on a lot of rage, then individual psychotherapy utilizing EMDR or somatic work with a focus on impulse control is indicated. Healing intensives such as the Hoffman Process, the Star Process, Re-evaluation Counseling, and other therapy groups can also facilitate working through a surplus of anger safely.

If we need extra help mastering the Path to Peace, this procedure can be taken to a couple counselor for help with practice—or we can attend a NewCouple seminar. Because a failed Path to Peace is often the result of transference, whatever professional we choose to work with must be skilled in addressing that phenomenon. If we have difficulties with negotiation or negotiable agreement-making, couple counseling is again advised.

If we have difficulty creating or articulating core agreements within our relationship—including those defining sexual and emotional exclusivity—both couple and individual counseling can be helpful. If we fear that we can't stand by our core agreements, individual psychotherapy with a codependence expert utilizing EMDR or somatic work addressing possible abandonment trauma, assertiveness training, self-empowerment courses, men's and women's groups, Codependents Anonymous, and healing intensives are all suggested.

Self-Love

If we're aware of deficit self-love—that is, we recognize our inability to trust our feelings and intuition, honor our talents, stick up for or care for ourselves, deidealize or individuate from family members, or work through the transference that comes up in our relationships—we can benefit from all forms of Help. On-going individual psychotherapy with a trusted therapist is among the most powerful interventions for low self-love; additionally, the Hoffman Process and the Star Process are highly recommended. Since low self-love can be the result of emotional trauma and growing up with addiction, abuse, and mental illness, Twelve-Step, therapy, and support groups addressing these problems can be invaluable. If as a couple we need facilitated practice identifying transferences, couple counseling is the place to learn. If we're unable to identify or recall the childhood relationship at the root of a transference or neutralize the associated feelings, these issues can all be addressed in individual and couple therapy.

Mission in Life

If we're confused about our true life's work and unsure where our greatest gifts and talents lie, we can be inestimably helped by a coach—whether job, life, personal, or dream variety. Life-mission, life-purpose, life-transition, and accountability support groups, as well as Speaking Circles, can open us up to our true calling, as can workshops concentrating on financial empowerment and mission in life. The Hoffman Process and the Star Process can be of particular merit too, especially if we specify identifying our mission as a workshop goal. If we suspect that low self-love is contributing to our confusion, the self-love suggestions above are also appropriate.

Walking

If we're unable or unwilling to consider leaving a relationship where our essential needs are unmet, we're suffering from emotional dependencies (or codependence within the relationship), financial dependencies, or both. If the dependencies are emotional, the same Help options mentioned in the codependence discussion (see "Priority," above) are appropriate. If the dependencies are financial, we can make great headway by attending courses designed for financial and personal empowerment, as well as for development of mission or purpose in life. Coaches can also be excellent resources to help get us up and running with our own money.

LOCATING RESOURCES MENTIONED IN THIS CHAPTER

The references and additional readings on the following pages in the area of Help is by no means exhaustive. For more information, search the Internet or ask for referrals from your church, hospital, physician, alternative healthcare practitioner, or friends.

THE KEY TO HELP

Being willing to do whatever learning and healing is necessary if you're stuck on any aspect of the first nine Natural Laws of Love is the key to the tenth Natural Law of Love.

RESOURCES, REFERENCE
and ADDITIONAL READING

NewCouple, Int'l.: (415) 332-8881; www.newcouple.com. Our organization offers NewCouple Seminars designed to accelerate participants' mastery of the concepts, skills, and processes described in this book in a safe, supportive environment. We also feature lectures and video/audiotapes based on the Ten Natural Laws of Love.

Institute for Imago Relationship Therapy (Harville Hendrix's Couple Workshops): (800) 729-1121; www.imagotherapy.com

Jewish Marriage Encounter: (800) 887-7544; www.jewishmarriage.org

Marriage Encounter: (800) 795-5683; www.wwm.org

The Star Foundation: (888) 857-STAR; www.starfound.org

The Hoffman Institute (USA): (800) 506-5253; www.hoffmaninstitute.org

The Hoffman Centre (Australia): 61-3-9826-2133; www.quadrinity.com

The Hoffman Centre (UK): 44-1903-88-99-90; www.quadrinity.com

Re-evaluation Counseling: (206) 284-0311; www.rc.org

The Primal Therapy Institute (Arthur Janov's Primal Center): (310) 392-2003; www.primaltherapy.com

Speaking Circles International: (800) 610-0169; www.speakingcircles.com

Impact Bay Area Self-Defense: (510) 208-0474; www.impactbayarea.org

The Twelve-Step programs listed below are widely available. In addition to the phone numbers and websites listed below, you can find such programs locally by referring to a phone book, therapist, hospital, or church.

Adult Children of Alcoholics (ACA/ACOA): (310) 534-1815; www.adultchildren.org

Al-Anon/Alateen (for family members and friends of alcoholics): (888) 4AL-ANON; www.al-anon.alateen.org

Alcoholics Anonymous (AA); AA World Services: (212) 870-3400; www.aa.org

Codependents Anonymous (CODA): (602) 277-7991; www.codependents.org

Debtors Anonymous (DA): (781-453-2743); wwwdebtorsanonymous.org

Gamblers Anonymous (GA): (213) 386-8789; www.gamblersanonymous.org

Narcotics Anonymous (NA): (818) 773-9999; www.na.org

199

Nar-Anon (for family members and friends of drug users): (310) 547-5800; www.naranon.org

Overeaters Anonymous (OA): (505) 891-2664; www.oa.org

Rational Recovery (Nonspiritual AA): (800) 303-2873

Recovering Couples Anonymous (RCA): (510) 663-2312; www.recovering-couples.org

Sex and Love Addicts Anonymous (SLAA): (210) 828-7900; www.slaafws.org

Survivors of Incest Anonymous (SIA): (410) 282-3400: www.siawso.org

Workaholics Anonymous (WA): (510) 273-9253; www.workaholics-anonymous.org

Bass, Ellen, and Laura Davis. *The Courage to Heal: A Guide for Women Survivors of Child Sexual Abuse.*

Beattie, Melody. *Codependent No More: How to Stop Controlling Others and Start Caring for Yourself.*

Bradshaw, John. *Healing the Shame That Binds You*

Bradshaw, John. *Bradshaw on the Family: A Revolutionary Way of Self-Discovery*

Carnes, Patrick. *Out of the Shadows: Understanding Sexual Addiction*

Gill, Merton. *The Analysis of Transference,* vol.1

Glickstein, Lee. *Be Heard Now! How to Tap into Your Inner Speaker and Communicate with Ease.*

Harris, Thomas. *I'm OK, You're OK.*

Hendrix, Harville. *Getting All the Love You Want: A Guide for Couples.*

Kahn, Michael. *Between Therapist and Client: The New Relationship*

Kohut, Heinz *How Doe Analysis Cure?*

Lee, John. *Growing Yourself Back Up: Understanding Emotional Regression.*

Levine, Peter A. *Waking the Tiger: Healing Trauma.*

Lew, Mike and Eileen Bass. *Victims No Longer: A Guide for Men Recovering from Sexual Child Abuse.*

Love, Patricia and Jo Robinson. *The Emotional Incest Syndrome: What to do When a Parent's Love Rules Your Life.*

Maslow, Abraham. *Toward the Psychology of Being.*

Mellody, Pia. *Facing Love Addiction*

Miller, Alice. *Drama of the Gifted Child*

Parnell, Laurel. *Transforming Trauma: EMDR*

Rogers, Carl. *On Becoming a Person.*

GLOSSARY

The following terms found throughout the book are essential to understanding the Ten Natural Laws of Love. The specific laws they relate to are listed in parentheses after each definition.

ACTING IN. The result of an unwillingness or inability to express feelings directly, acting in involves turning our negative feelings self-abusively against ourselves. Acting in, which is a response to feelings of toxic guilt and toxic shame, is typically experienced as "beating ourselves up." It often leads to codependence, compulsions, and addictions, our unconscious attempts to dull the pain of self-abuse. (EMOTIONAL INTEGRITY AND PEACEMAKING)

ACTING OUT. The unhealthy expression of feelings, especially anger and fear. Examples of acted-out anger include sarcasm, bullying, and punishing silence; examples of acted-out fear include controlling behaviors, false joy and kindness, and general overcaution. (EMOTIONAL INTEGRITY and PEACEMAKING)

AGGRESSIVE-AGGRESSIVE BEHAVIOR. The more overt and direct form of acted-out anger, aggressive-aggressive behavior includes verbal abuse, coercion, threats, throwing and breaking things, and violence. (EMOTIONAL INTEGRITY AND PEACEMAKING)

AMENDS. A part of the negotiable agreement–making process, amends represent favors or gestures offered to our partner when we break a negotiable agreement. (PEACEMAKING)

ANGER MANAGEMENT. A commitment to neither act out ourselves nor tolerate the acting out of anger by our partner and a commitment to use the time-out anger-management tool are at the heart of anger management. (PEACEMAKING)

CO-CREATIVITY. The final stage of relationship, co-creativity is characterized by interdependence, emotional intimacy, rising self-love, and activated dual missions in life. The traditional couple didn't typically arrive at co-creativity, because the help necessary to resolve the power struggle wasn't available. (IDENTIFY and all laws)

CODEPENDENCE. The unhealthy preoccupation with another person, codependence often leads us to place others' needs before our own or to seek others' acceptance before we accept ourselves. Like all compulsive behaviors, codependence is an attempt to avoid our own pain. (IDENTIFY , PRIORITY, EMOTIONAL INTEGRITY, SELF-LORE, WALKING)

CONDITIONAL SELF-LOVE. A false kind of self-love, conditional self-love is based on external factors, such as money, looks, credentials, or talent, while genuine self-love is based on our ability to love ourselves regardless. (SELF-LOVE)

CORE AGREEMENTS / CORE CONDITIONS. Tools and part of the peacemaking technology, core agreements are a couple's nonnegotiable agreements based on each individual partner's core conditions—the individual partners' nonnegotiable conditions for relationship. Core agreements/core conditions are nonviolence, monogamy with sexual exclusivity, honesty, all forms of sobriety, and noncriminality, as well as a commitment to the Ten Laws. Core conditions are determined on an individual basis.(PEACEMAKING)

EIGHTY/TWENTY PRINCIPLE. This principle reflects the fact that roughly eighty percent of the emotional charge involved in major couple conflicts derives from transference—that is, unresolved hurts from early caregivers and siblings—while roughly twenty percent derives from the contemporary situation with our partner. (SELF-LOVE)

EMOTIONAL NUMBNESS. An emotional blind spot resulting in our inability to feel emotion in the moment, numbness is typically a consequence of unresolved childhood trauma. (EMOTIONAL INTEGRITY)

EMOTIONAL SAFE ZONE. A relationship environment in which we feel no fear of being emotionally invalidated, lied to, or intentionally hurt. Emotional safe zones free us to be our most emotionally honest, expressive, and authentic selves. (CHEMISTRY, EMOTIONAL INTEGRITY, PEACEMAKING, and SELF-LOVE)

HEALTHY GUILT. Based on a bona fide violation of another, healthy guilt produces healthy results, including discouraging repetition of the transgression and teaching trustworthiness. (EMOTIONAL INTEGRITY)

HEALTHY SHAME. Based on a reasonable self-protective concern for the high regard of others, healthy shame produces healthy results, such as keeping us from behaving in ways that would result in social rejection (which few of us have the self-love to tolerate). (EMOTIONAL INTEGRITY)

INDIVIDUATION. Integral to prioritizing our relationship, individuation is the process of becoming a psychological adult *vis-a-vis* parents and other early caregivers, siblings, and extended family members. We can determine our level of individuation by the degree to which we assert our own authority with family members. If we're driven by the need for their approval or by the fear of disappointing, hurting, angering, or being rejected by them, we haven't yet completed the individuation process. (PRIORITY)

I-STATEMENTS. Facilitating the direct and healthy expression of emotion using the "I feel" format. I-statements are key to emotional fluency and emotional management. (EMOTIONAL INTEGRITY)

NEGOTIABLE AGREEMENTS. Part of the peacemaking technology, negotiable agreements are a conflict-resolution tool. They're designed to address issues not covered by core agreements. (PEACEMAKING)

NEW COUPLE. Any couple that actively and mutually embraces the higher-order needs for self-love, mission in life, and emotional intimacy is a "New Couple." (IDENTIFY and all laws)

GLOSSARY

PARENTAL IDEALIZATION. An early childhood need to see our parents as perfect and completely competent caregivers, parental idealization often carries over into adulthood. It is the biggest challenge to resolving transference, because overcoming it usually involves moving through fear and grief. Arrested parental idealization is the result of unresolved childhood emotional trauma and exacerbates transference with our partner. (SELF LOVE)

PASSIVE-AGGRESSIVE BEHAVIOR. The indirect and covert form of acted-out anger, passive-aggressive behavior includes victim talk, patronization, sarcasm, teasing, denial, withdrawal, "forgetting," and sabotage. (EMOTIONAL INTEGRITY and PEACEMAKING)

PATH TO PEACE. The New Couple conflict-resolution tool. (PEACEMAKING)

PROCESS ADDICTION. Unlike substance addiction, which involves the consumption of an addictive substance, process addiction is the inability to stop certain behaviors, such as work, sexual activity (or preoccupation), and gambling, despite harm to one or more of the core areas of our lives—namely, health, livelihood, and primary relationships. (PRIORITY)

SHAME SEIZURE. The sudden, overwhelming experience of toxic shame is known as a shame seizure. (EMOTIONAL INTEGRITY)

TOXIC GUILT. An unhealthy emotion, toxic guilt results when we unfairly accuse ourselves of being responsible for the emotional well-being of another. It's a key characteristic of codependence. (EMOTIONAL INTEGRITY)

TOXIC SHAME. An unhealthy emotion, toxic shame results from the erroneous belief that we're inherently inadequate and unlovable; this leads to an unreasonable fear of being exposed as such to others. Along with toxic guilt, toxic shame is a key characteristic of codependence. (EMOTIONAL INTEGRITY)

TRANSFERENCE. A case of mistaken identity, transference results when we unconsciously confuse our partner with those with whom we grew up. This leads us to emotionally "transfer" the role of primary caregiver or sibling onto our partner. Any button, blind spot, or issue that requires use of the time-out tool indicates transference (and probably involves unresolved trauma as well). Resolving transference requires that we seek to identify and work through our feelings about the original relationship that hurt us, a process that enhances our self-love. (SELF-LOVE)

TRIANGLE TEST. Part of the peacemaking technology, the Triangle Test helps us determine whether or not we're ready for a successful Path to Peace. It features our three subpersonalities: the Adult, the Child, and the Critic. (PEACEMAKING)

WRITTEN PATH TO PEACE. Part of the peacemaking technology and a conflict-resolution tool, the written Path to Peace is usually used when the verbal Path to Peace has failed. (PEACEMAKING)

INDEX

MAURICE TAYLOR and SEANA McGEE, a married couple, are licensed psychotherapists specializing in couple counseling. They are internationally known relationship experts and founding directors of NewCouple, Int'l., a seminar and lecture organization for couples and singles. They live in Sausalito, California on a houseboat with the Golden Gate Bridge in view.

COLOPHON
The text was set in Garamond, a typeface designed by Claude Garamond (1500-1561). The typeface, Garamond, is a reworking of Aldus Manutius' *De Aetna*. The display faces are various forms of Gill Sans and the folios are Sabon SC. *What's the State of Your Union?* was typeset by Rhode Island Book Composition, Kingston, Rhode Island and printed by Versa Press, East Peoria, Illinois on acid-free paper.